Essence of Systems Analysis and Design

Priti Srinivas Sajja

Essence of Systems Analysis and Design

A Workbook Approach

 Springer

Priti Srinivas Sajja
PG Department of Computer Science
Sardar Patel University
Vallabh Vidyanagar, Gujarat, India

ISBN 978-981-13-5326-0   ISBN 978-981-10-5128-9   (eBook)
DOI 10.1007/978-981-10-5128-9

Printed on acid-free paper

This Springer imprint is published by Springer Nature
The registered company is Springer Nature Singapore Pte Ltd.
The registered company address is: 152 Beach Road, #21-01/04 Gateway East, Singapore 189721,
Singapore

Preface

A system is a ubiquitous phenomenon. From early learning activities to the spectacular education and practices, one has to deal with systems. The subject of systems analysis and design has been taught to various streams, courses, and levels. There are many careers that require a fundamental knowledge of the subject. To name a few, software engineer, tester, systems analyst, programmer, designer, knowledge engineer, data scientists, and Big Data practitioner are the roles where systems analysis and design knowledge is a must. Rather, it can be said that in all aspects of the business, somewhere the subject is useful.

As a teacher of the systems analysis and design subject at the postgraduate level, I have observed following important things:

- The systems analysis and design subject is very lengthy and descriptive in nature, which confuse students about the applicability of answers.
- Quick revision from the reference book is challenging.
- Supporting materials such as diagrams, case studies, and objective as well as subjective questions with answers are also not available in a single book.

The book *Essence of Systems Analysis and Design – A Workbook Approach* identifies essential topics and presents cruxes of the core topics, which are mandatory and trivial. Further, the book encompasses questions and answers based on the selected topics. The main objective of the book is to provide quick and essential knowledge for the subject with the help of summary and solved questions/case studies without going into detail discussion of the content. This book will be much helpful for the students as a supplementary text-/workbook and to the noncomputer professionals, who deal with the systems analysis and design as part of their business. The problem-solving approach of the book enables learners, academicians, practitioners, and researchers to gain much practical knowledge of the subject, without going into lengthy discussions. Besides quick understanding of the core topics via practical problem solving, this book also provides guidance on how to document answers and cases related to the subject.

Though the book is conceived as the supplementary text-/workbook, the topics are selected and arranged in such a way that it can provide complete and sufficient knowledge of the subject. Graduate courses like BSc (computer science), BCA, BE, BBA, BCom, and BA (humanities such as economics and cooperation) and post-graduate courses such as MSc/MS, MCA, M-eBusiness, ME, etc. along with some interdisciplinary and certificate courses can use this book for a quick and ready reference of systems analysis and design.

I would like to thank the Almighty for giving me strength, opportunity, and blessings for the book. I am very much thankful to students and colleagues at the Department of Computer Science, Sardar Patel University, especially Sanskruti Patel, who have encouraged me to come up with this novel book. I would like to express my sincere thanks to Suvira Srivastava, Yeshmeena Bisht, Sanchana Narayanassamy and Abha Krishnan for their continuous support during the book publication. Thanks to Srinivas and Abhignya for their continuous support and encouragement.

Vallabh Vidyanagar, India   Priti Srinivas Sajja

Contents

About the Author

Dr. Priti Srinivas Sajja has been working at the Post Graduate Department of Computer Science, Sardar Patel University, India, since 1994 and presently holds the post of Professor. She specializes in artificial intelligence and systems analysis and design and has produced over 180 publications, which include seven books and eleven book chapters. She is the co-author of *Intelligent Techniques for Data Science* (Springer, 2016); *Intelligent Technologies for Web Applications* (CRC Press, 2012) and *Knowledge-Based Systems* (J&B, 2009) published in Switzerland and the USA, and four books published in India. Further, she has served as Principal Investigator of a major research project funded by the University Grants Commission, India.

Chapter 1
Introductory Concepts of Systems Analysis and Design

Abstract This chapter introduces basic concepts of systems analysis and design. System is a ubiquitous phenomenon. The chapter introduces the concept of systems with its general diagram and discusses its prime components along with various categories of systems. The discussed categories are Transaction Processing Systems (TPS), Management Information System (MIS), Decision Support System (DSS), and Expert System (ES) besides open and closed systems. Further, data pyramid (DIKW hierarchy) is also discussed with various levels of users and systems including total information system. After having a brief discussion of systems components and various categories of systems with real-life examples, systems analysis and design is defined along with duties and roles of Systems Analyst. To develop an information system, many approaches are used; prime of them are Systems Development Life Cycle (SDLC) approach, structured approach, and prototype approach which are briefly discussed. To manage the systems development process, the role of Systems Analyst and various committees is introduced in this chapter. The chapter also discusses need and reasons of systems development considering broad as well as detailed reasons in terms of five Cs, namely, cost, capacity, control, communication, and competitive advantages. To efficiently manage the development-related activities, concept of portfolio is discussed. The chapter also enlists tools for systems development at end. Exercise/practice questions with answers and objective questions (multiple choice) with solutions are also provided.

© Springer Nature Singapore Pte Ltd. 2017
P.S. Sajja, *Essence of Systems Analysis and Design*,
DOI 10.1007/978-981-10-5128-9_1

1.1   Introduction

System is a ubiquitous phenomenon. Systems are everywhere. If something is systematic, it yields qualitative results. From early learning activities to the spectacular specialized education and practice, one has to deal with systems. We have seen and experienced real-life systems such as education system, political system, digestive system, weather forecasting system, tickets reservation system, fault finding system, workflow management system, and admission system. This chapter provides summary of systems introductory topics such as generic systems, components of a system, categories of systems, data pyramid, systems analysis, systems design, systems development, roles and duties of Systems Analyst, etc. along with various systems development methodologies.

1.2   System and Its Components

A system is a collection of different components that work together to achieve some objectives. These components must work in harmony with each other to accomplish the predefined goals. The typical components about a system are input, processing, output, and decision-making mechanisms. Boundary is the concept which separates the system from its environment. Sometimes, for a system, boundary acts as an interface to interact with the environment related to the system.

1.2.1   Open and Closed Systems

A system that interacts with its environment is called an open system. In opposite, a system that does not interact with its environment is called a closed system. Closed systems are just like a black box or an insulated container. Since it is not accepting anything from its environment and not returning anything to the environment, closed system will not serve an objective of a typical business. Most of the businesses are meant for profit, job satisfaction (in terms of appreciation of service) and entertainment. A closed system never earns any of these. That is why most of the real-life systems (as mentioned in Sect. 1) are open systems.

1.2.2   Components of a System

As stated above, there are three major components in every system, namely, input, processes (or processing), and output. Fig. 1.1 illustrates these major components.

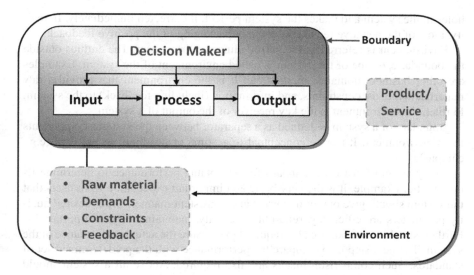

Fig. 1.1 Components of a typical system

Input includes those elements and information that are provided to the system. Typical inputs to a system can be raw material, information related to demand, government-/authority-imposed rules and regulations, customers' feedback, and environmental or business constraints.

Set of processes is the component which is mainly responsible to process and convert the given inputs into the desired forms. This component encompasses broad outline of major procedures in order to convert into the suitable output.

Output is the amount of the information, product (finished or semifinished), or work provided by the system after processing given inputs. Output generally describes/delivers the finished products through a system. The output is meant for the systems user. Examples of output are services, finished products, or profit.

Feedback is the information provided back to the system. Typically feedback comes from environment in case of open system. Once output of a system reaches to its intended users (which may be internal or external users), the users might share important information with the system in return. It can be appreciation (for a really good system), errors, questions and clarification requests, some more demands, and information. There are two types of feedback: positive feedback and negative feedback.

Positive feedback encourages the developer, management, and other users to use the system and increases the degree of systems acceptance among users. Positive feedback generally comes in terms of appreciation and sometimes with more demands and requirements.

Negative feedback generally reports about bugs and faults in the system. The early negative feedback (if taken positively!) identifies many limitations and loopholes in the system and makes the system perfect, if corrected immediately. In reality, most of the negative feedbacks come in packaging of the positive feedback.

Environment is referred as the surroundings of the system. The entities outside the boundaries/scope of the system is called environment of the system. Examples are other business domains, market, etc. It is the environment that provides raw material, demands, constraints, and information (including feedback) to the system. Further, the environment is the key receiver of the output of a system.

Boundary of a system is defined as a separator between the systems components to its environment. It can be conceptual (e.g., time or deadline) or physical (e.g., campus).

Every system must have standard for acceptable performance to determine its quality. For example, it is the very basic and important expectation from users that the system should give output in correct and consistent manner. Other desired quality parameters are efficiency, reliability, usability, maintainability, and portability. Further, suitable methods are also required to measure the actual performance of the system. The next step is to compare the performance with the predetermined set of standards. Such comparison means are also required. Above all a system should have a method of feedback also.

Let us take an example of body mass index (BMI) calculation. The formula for calculating BMI is needed, which is a method to judge the actual value (performance). The formula is as follows:

$$\text{BMI} = \left\{ \text{weight} \left(\text{in pounds} \right)^* .45 \right\} / \text{height squared} \left(\text{in centimeters} \right).$$

A standard BMI value to the target user is also needed. The well-defined standards for BMI are as follows:

BMI categories   Underweight = <18.5
Normal weight = 18.5–24.9
Overweight = 25–29.9
Obesity = BMI of 30 or greater

We also require means of comparison, such that less than, greater than, equal to, etc.

At the end, it is also important to have method of feedback that less BMI is better or more BMI is better and in which category the calculated BMI lies.

1.3   Information Systems and Data Pyramid

The data pyramid is a model that encompasses different hierarchical levels of data, information, knowledge, wisdom, and intelligence along with various information systems associated with it. It is also known as DIKW pyramid or DIKW hierarchy. According to the data pyramid, data are very trivial entities and form base of the

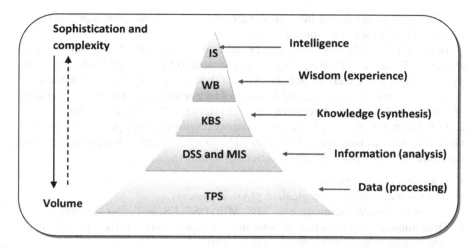

Fig. 1.2 Data pyramid

data pyramid. Data are defined as raw observations. Often, data are known as facts, symbols, or signals. Once data are collected and processed, information is generated. Data processing is the key operation that converts the data into information. Information has a factor of usability and meaning associated with it, whereas standalone data are of not much use. Sufficient amount of information is processed and synthesized to create knowledge. The acquired pieces of knowledge are evaluated in terms of time, experience, and ethics in order to generate wisdom. At the end, with similar practice, intelligence is generated. Fig. 1.2 illustrates data pyramid and related information systems in it.

As illustrated in Fig. 1.2, each section has its corresponding information systems too. An information system is a collection of hardware, software, data, people, and procedures that are designed to generate information that supports the day-to-day as well as long-range activities of users in an organization.

Data occupies the base of the pyramid as shown in Fig. 1.2. It is voluminous in comparison with other compartments. At this lower level, very structured and predefined systems work. Such systems are known as Transaction Processing Systems (TPS). Mostly, lower-level users (also called end users) are using the system.

At the next level, within the information compartment of the pyramid, two systems operate, namely, Management Information Systems (MIS) and Decision Support Systems (DSS). The MIS provides routine as well as exceptional information to the management in systematic forms (reports). The DSS works a step ahead. It applies models from the system's model base and suggests possible alternatives accordingly. Middle-level and strategic-level management is using these systems. At knowledge level Expert Systems (ES), which is a Knowledge Based System (KBS), and at wisdom level Wisdom-Based Systems (WBS) are working. At top of the pyramid, Intelligent Systems (IS) are placed (Akerkar and Sajja 2009).

When you go up within the DIKW hierarchy, the volume decreases and complexity as well as sophistication increases.

Besides TPS, MIS, DSS, ES, and IS, other categories of information systems also exist. These include Office Automation Systems (OAS), Executive Information System (EIS), and Executive Support System (ESS). One may think of hybrid category of systems by incorporating features of two or more categories. An example of such hybrid system is Executive Expert System (EES), which is fusion of ESS and ES. Further, many people classify systems according to their processing mechanism also, such as batch processing, real-time processing, and distributed processing. Here are a few possible classifications of systems:

- Open and closed systems
- Abstract/conceptual, biological, or physical systems
- As per the DIKW hierarchy, e.g., TPS, MIS, DSS, ES, and other systems
- Deterministic system (where actions are known with certainty) and probabilistic system (occurrence of an event is not certain)
- Hard computing systems (with rigid procedures and logic) and soft computing (approximate and fuzzy logic)
- As per applications or working such as manufacturing, service, geographic, marketing and promotion, planning, monitoring and control, governance, etc.

It is obvious that a business is also thought as an information system. Rather, every business can be abstracted in form of an information system. Many systems can simultaneously exist at different levels of an organization. However, a single information system that meets the needs of an organization at various levels and across many business functions is also possible. Such information system is known as total information system.

1.4   Users of System

Persons who directly or indirectly use the system are identified as users or end users. Table 1.1 enlists four types of users.

Besides these typical users as shown in Table 1.1, system developers such as Systems Analyst, programmers, and testers are also users of the system.

Table 1.1 Users of system

Users	Description
Direct users	Hands on end users such as operators and clerks who directly work with the system
Indirect users	Use the system indirectly through the reports or output provided by the system. Example can be supervisors and sectional heads
Managers	Use system for overall control and organizational responsibilities
Strategic and top-level users	Take responsibilities of strategic planning and risk evaluation

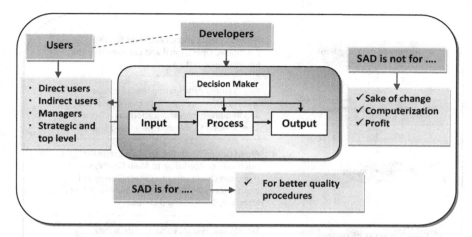

Fig. 1.3 System, users, and reasons for systems analysis and design

1.5   Systems Analysis and Design

It is not necessary that every system must be computerized system. A system can be noncomputer-based system. The basic objective of doing the systems analysis and design is to develop better procedures for business. The systems analysis and design should not be carried out for profit, for the sake of changing the existing system, or for computerization. However, these all can be the by-products of the systems analysis and design practice. Fig. 1.3 describes various users, typical systems components, systems developers, and reasons to go for systems analysis and design.

Systems analysis and design together is known as systems development. The systems analysis phase is defined as a process of gathering and interpreting facts, diagnosing problems, and using the information to recommend improvements to the system. The systems design deals with how this improvement (generally in form of requirements) can be achieved.

A system can be developed using a well-defined approaches and models. Systems Development Life Cycle (SDLC – also known as the classical approach), structured approach, and prototype are other examples of the major approaches to develop a system.

1.6   Systems Development Life Cycle Approach

This approach is also known as classical approach to develop a system. This approach consists of different phases which need to be completed in strict sequential order. That is why the approach is called linear approach. The phases are shown with their related activities in form of Fig. 1.4. The brief discussion about the phases involved in this approach is discussed in practice question 1.15.14.

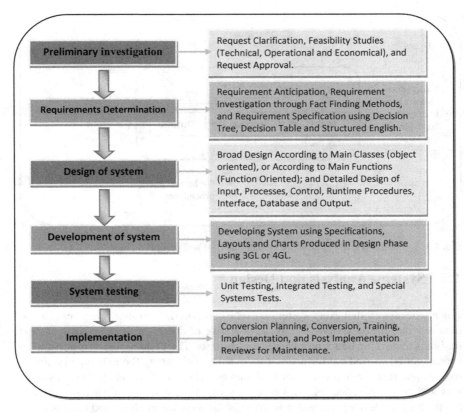

Fig. 1.4 SDLC (classical) model with its phases and activities

The limitation of this model is that, once a phase is completed, you cannot go back. That means, the requirements and design once determined, cannot be changed in between.

1.7 Structured Analysis and Design Approach

This approach focuses systematic development of a system in very organized way. The basic objective of this approach is to manage big and complex system by dividing it into modules. This facilitates parallel development of the system as well as better control with ease of development. The main characteristic of the approach is its dependency on graphical tools. If the system is divided according to main classes in it, Unified Modeling Language (UML) is used to facilitate study of existing system's design during the analysis phase and to develop proposed system's design (object oriented approach). Otherwise, if the system is broken into modules

according to main functions in it, function decomposition diagrams (FDDs or structured charts) and data flow diagrams (DFDs) are used (functional or structured
approach). These concepts are discussed at Chap. 3.

1.8   Prototype Approach

Prototype is defined as live, working model of the system. Before actual systems
development, a working model of the system is developed in this approach in quick
and iterative fashion. The prototype is then used to warm up users, to collect more
requirements, to demonstrate expected features of the system, and to test feasibility
of the system before actually developing it. If prototype is good enough, it can be
revised and accepted as a full-fledged system. For the novel and risky systems or
systems with partial list of requirements, the prototype is suitable approach. The
concept of prototype is discussed in detail at Chap. 4.

1.9   Roles and Duties of Systems Analyst

In a big organization, dedicated resources and experts to perform various duties are
made available. Systems Analyst has to perform analysis only. Systems Analyst
here plays a role of visionary and leads organization toward better systems.

The duties of a Systems Analyst in a medium firm are to analyze and provide
design of the system. In a small organization, the duties of Systems Analyst cover a
big span. He has to do analysis, design, and programming.

Systems Analyst is a motivator to develop or modify the systems at the organizations and brings positive change by suggesting quality procedures in the business
for foreseeing the future.

1.10   End User and Institutional Approaches of Systems
Development

In the end user systems development approach, the responsibility to develop an
application is in the hands of end user. The selected end users need to be directly
involved with all development phases, including requirement determination. The
end users are supposed to do the following:

- End user must understand the business problem.
- End users often have to do the market survey for ready-made solutions and available tools.

- They should collect data limited to the business problem and prepare the data for further processing.
- They should have knowledge of user-friendly software packages which are suitable for the system. Systems Analyst can provide guidance to the end users in this process.
- End users also identify suitable quality standards, protocols, and metrics with the help of Systems Analyst.
- End users are responsible to develop and install system for use.
- End users are also responsible for necessary documentation, training, and conversion of the system.

It is responsibility of the Systems Analyst to guide end users in terms of finding suitable tools and quality standards for the system.

Institutional approach of systems development considers systems which are affecting the whole organization instead of a limited domain or set of users. That is, the systems which are broader in scope and/or affecting basic objective of the business are the candidates for this approach. For example, applications such as income tax planning system or employee attendance system are applicable to all employees of the organization. Instead of going for end user development approach, a systematic institutional approach needs to be followed. Here, Systems Analyst and his team (or any Systems Development Committee) take the responsibility for the systems development.

1.11 Information Systems Development Committees

Often it is believed that it is Systems Analyst's duty to develop and implement full system with the help of information/computer section in an organization. This is true, especially when the Systems Analyst himself has envisioned a new, better quality system or the organization is very small. Besides the Systems Analysts and information section in the organization, users themselves can also develop systems, as stated above in an end user development approach. Another alternative is to go for outsourcing and consultancy to develop the system through the professional agencies. The last approach is the steering committee approach. Such committee will comprise of computer personnel such as Systems Analyst, programmers, and testers; management personnel from administration, accounts, and higher authority, especially skilled people such as graphic designer, hardware engineer, etc.; and a few users. Inclusion of variety of flavors in the development committee ensures smooth development procedures. Table 1.2 enlists these approaches.

Table 1.2 Systems development committees

Committee	Description
Information Systems Group	Responsibility of development of system is solely on the information systems group under leadership of Systems Analyst
Users Group	End users are responsible to develop the system
Consultancy/Outside Group	Systems development responsibilities are on the shoulders of outside group
Steering Committee	Computer personnel (Systems Analyst, programmers, etc.); management personnel from various sections, especially skilled people (graphic designer, hardware engineer, etc.); and a few users are involved to facilitate smooth development of the system

1.12 Reasons for Systems Development

Development of a new system can be proposed by Systems Analyst, authority, end users, or any third party. The broad objectives of the systems development are given in Table 1.3. Senn (2008) provided detail discussions on these objectives.

The other aspects such as cost of the systems development as well as maintenance, capacity of the system, etc. also need to be considered. These aspects are well defined in the work of Senn (2008) which are summarized in Table 1.4 with a brief description of each parameter.

1.13 Systems Portfolio and Portfolio Integration

Systems portfolio in an organization is a collection of information systems or activities related to the development, which are in pipeline for development or currently being developed. When a proposal comes for development of a system, it will undergo the request clarification, preliminary investigation, and feasibility analysis. After employing these activities, if the system seems to be worth for development, it will be included in the portfolio. Each organization or a section with the organization has at least one such portfolio. The portfolio facilitates the future view of the organization or section (the portfolio also provides facility to foresee near future of an organization). Different sections and organizations may share their respective portfolios for sharing their development views and mission. Table 1.5 enlists different ways of portfolio sharing.

1.14 Tools for Systems Development

During analysis the emphasis is given to collect as many as facts related to the system. For the analysis purpose, dictionary, charting, and data collection tools are helpful. During the design phase, graphical tools like UML (Unified Modeling

Table 1.3 Broad reasons for new systems development

Objective	Description
To solve a problem	New system may be developed to solve problems with the existing system. It can be a new technology or new requirements, which the existing system cannot cope up
To utilize opportunities	Since ample amount of expertise, raw material, side products, and experience are earned via the existing system, it is advisable to go for extension of business and extend the system in a suitable way. Sometimes, a new system is conceived in such a way that the existing system acts as a subsystem of the new system
To meet authority demands	The authority might have envisioned the future requirement of information system and has demanded for a new system

Table 1.4 Other reasons for new systems development (five Cs)

Objective	Description
To save the running and maintaining cost of the business	New system is often developed to cut off the cost of business by including new procedures in the proposed system. Cost monitoring of the business activities can also be an objective of a new system
To increase the working capacity of the system	Capacity of a system can be enhanced by increasing the speed of processing through new procedures and techniques. The new system can also be developed so that it can handle large volume of transactions of the business. It will also process transactions and output reports efficiently
To improve the control on systems procedures	New system can be enriched with secured procedures and increased consistency in order to get better control on the business activities. Having better control often leads to increased consistency, improved quality, and effectiveness to the business
To enforce better communication	To facilitate smooth and efficient flow between various business components, new system can be proposed. It can integrate various business areas and provides opportunities of integration of various business activities
To take competitive advantages	New system is often required to attract users and maintain them to compete with competitors. New procedures, services, and products may be introduced to do so

Language, which is a generic modeling language to visualize the design of a system) and specification and layout tools are helpful. During development code generators, testing tools and Computer-Aided Software/System Engineering (CASE) tools such as IBM's Rational Rose[1] are used.

---

[1] http://www-03.ibm.com/software/products/en/enterprise

Table 1.5 Various portfolio integration paradigms

Type of integration	Description
Horizontal	Two sections in an organization or two organizations at same level may share their systems portfolio to reduce development burden and to learn from the sister concerns
Vertical	Small subsection or an organization may share its portfolio to the parent institute to report and combine the current and future activities of the organization
Physical	Integration of portfolios of the organization which spans geographic boundaries
External	Sharing portfolio of an internal business with a portfolio of an external business

1.15 Practice Questions

1.15.1 What Is System? Define Elements of System. Give Example and Description of Each in Brief. Also, Draw the Structure Diagram of the System

A system is a set of different components that work together to achieve some objectives. These components must work in harmony with each other to accomplish the predefined goals.

The typical components of a system are input, processing, output, and decision-making mechanisms. Boundary is the concept which separates the system from its environment. Sometimes, for a system, boundary acts as an interface to interact with the environment related to the system. Refer Fig. 1.1.

Brief description of the each component is given below.

Input Includes those elements and information that are provided to the system. Typical inputs to a system can be raw material, information related to demand, government-/authority-imposed rules and regulations, customers' feedback, and environmental or business constraints.

Processes Set of processes is the component which is mainly responsible to process and convert the given inputs into the desired forms. This component encompasses broad outline of major procedures in order to convert into the suitable output.

Output Is the amount of the information, product (finished or semifinished), or services provided by the system after processing given inputs. Output generally describes/delivers the finished products through a system. The output is meant for the systems user. Examples of output are services, finished products, or profit.

Feedback Is the information provided back to the system. Typically feedback comes from environment in case of open system. Once output of a system reaches to its intended users (which may be internal or external users), the users might share important information with the system in return. It can be appreciation (for a really good system), errors, questions and clarification requests, some more demands, and information. There are two types of feedback: positive feedback and negative feedback.

Positive Feedback   Encourages the developer, management, and other users to use the system and increases the degree of systems acceptance among users. Positive feedback generally comes in terms of appreciation and sometimes with more demands and requirements.

Negative Feedback   Generally reports about bugs and faults in the system. The early negative feedback (if taken positively!) identifies many limitations and loopholes in the system and makes the system perfect, if corrected immediately. In reality, most of the negative feedbacks come in packaging of the positive feedback.

Environment   Is referred as the surroundings of the system. The entities outside the boundaries/scope of the system is called environment of the system. Examples are other business domains, market, suppliers, retailers, competitors, customers, authoring bodies (providing standards), etc. It is the environment that provides raw material, demands, constraints, and information (including feedback) to the system. Further, the environment is the key receiver of the output of a system.

Boundary   Boundary of a system is defined as a separator between the systems components and its environment. It can be conceptual (e.g., time or deadline) or physical (e.g., campus).

1.15.2   Differentiate Open and Closed Systems

Table 1.6   Difference between open and closed systems

Open system	Closed system
Interacts with its environment	Does not interact with its environment
Exchanges material, information such as feedback with its environment	Does not exchange material, information such as feedback with its environment
Most of the business systems are open systems	Closed system cannot be a typical real-life business system but a kind of self-organized entity
Open systems are adaptive and tend to react to the environment inputs	Closed system does not react (even does not interact) to its environment

1.15.3   What Is the Importance of Feedback? What Types of Feedback Do You Know?

Feedback is the information provided back to the system. Typically feedback comes from environment in case of open system. Once output of a system reaches to its intended users (which may be internal or external users), the users might share important information with the system in return. It can be appreciation (for a really good system), errors, questions and clarification requests, some more demands, and information. There are two types of feedback – positive and negative.

Positive Feedback Encourages the developer, management, and other users to use the system and increases the degree of systems acceptance among users. Positive feedback generally comes in terms of appreciation and sometimes with more demands and requirements.

Negative Feedback Generally reports about bugs and faults in the system. The early negative feedback (if taken positively!) identifies many limitations and loop-holes in the system and makes the system perfect, if corrected immediately. In reality, most of the negative feedbacks come in packaging of the positive feedback.

1.15.4 What Is Data Pyramid? Draw Data Pyramid. Show Data, Information, Knowledge, Wisdom, and Intelligence in It. Also Show Volume, Complexity, and Sophistication in the Pyramid

The data pyramid is a model that illustrates different hierarchical levels of data, information, knowledge, wisdom, and intelligence along with various information systems associated with it. It is also known as DIKW pyramid or DIKW hierarchy. According to the data pyramid, data are very trivial entities and form basis of the data pyramid. Data are defined as raw observations. Often, data are known as facts, symbols, or signals. Once data are collected and processed, information is generated. Data processing is the key operation that converts the data into information. Information has a factor of usability associated with it, whereas stand-alone data are of not much use. Sufficient amount of information is processed and synthesized to create knowledge. The acquired pieces of knowledge are evaluated in terms of time, experience, and ethics in order to generate wisdom. At the end, intelligence is generated in similar manner. When you go up in the data pyramid, the complexity and sophistication increase while volume decreases.

Refer to Fig. 1.2 which illustrates data pyramid and related information systems.

1.15.5 Discuss Various Types of an Information System with Brief Description of Each

Office Automation System (OAS)
An office automation system is a system designed to support routine and generic office activities of a typical organization. OAS automates and supports the tedious work of officers.

Transaction Processing System (TPS)

TPS deals with routine data transactions at lower-level management. Such transactions include reservation, deposit, withdraw, payment, etc. TPS works in very predefined and structured environment. TPS has to follow procedures and rules blindly without any decision-making. TPS mainly uses databases and files. Because of these characteristics, a TPS is comparatively easy to develop and automate.

Management Information System (MIS)

Management Information System (MIS) focuses on middle- to high-level management to increase the efficiency in structured representation of information. MIS works on underlying TPS. Typically a TPS processes data whereas an MIS generates informative reports based on this transaction processing. An MIS outputs generally provides routine reports and exceptional reports. MIS is semi-structured in nature. MIS also utilizes databases and files.

Decision Support System (DSS)

A Decision Support System (DSS) is a kind of information system that supports decision-making process of its users. DSS uses the systems model base to apply models on situations and provides a few alternatives with the respective cost–benefit statement. Statistical and operation research models are generally used along with the DSS. Such system also needs data from files or databases to keep factual information and temporary results. Many DSS can use online distributed databases or large warehouses to support decision-making process. DSS works in semi-structured to unstructured environment.

Expert System (ES)

Expert System (ES) is a system that works as an expert in given narrow domain using techniques of artificial intelligence. ES works in an unstructured environment. Expert system encompasses knowledge from various recourses including domain experts and preserves it into knowledge base, hence called KBS. Besides the knowledge base, an ES also uses databases and files. These systems are capable of taking decision with explanation and reasoning. ES can learn from cases and knowledge stored in knowledge bases.

1.15.6   What Is Total Information System?

A single information system that meets the needs of an organization at various levels and across many business functions is also possible; such information system is known as *total information system*.

1.15.7   Differentiate TPS and MIS

Table 1.7   Difference between TPS and MIS

TPS	MIS
Transaction Processing Systems process routine transactions in an organization	Management Information System (MIS) operates on the processed transactions and generates routine and exceptional reports
TPS work in predefined and structured way at lower-level management	MIS work in structured to semi-structured environment at middle-level and supervisory-level management
TPS processes data and outputs the signal of successful completion of transactions and/or error if any	MIS outputs routine and exceptional reports

1.15.8   Differentiate TPS and DSS

Table 1.8   Difference between TPS and DSS

TPS	DSS
Transaction Processing Systems (TPS) process routine transactions in an organization	Decision Support Systems (DSS) support decision-making procedures at middle to top management by suggesting various alternatives with cost–benefit ratio
TPS work in predefined and structured way at lower level of management	DSS work in semi-structured to unstructured environment at strategic-level and top-level management
TPS processes data and outputs the signal of successful completion of transactions and/or error, if any	DSS outputs alternative actions and decision with respective cost–benefit ratio

1.15.9   List Users of an Information System. Explain Each Category in Brief. Also Provide Example of Users in Each Category

Direct Users   Hands on end users such as operators and clerks who directly work with the system.

Indirect Users   Uses the system indirectly through the reports or output provided by the system. Example can be supervisors and sectional heads.

Managers   Uses system for overall control and organizational responsibilities such as general manager, chief executive, etc. of an organization.

Strategic and Top-Level Users   Takes responsibilities of strategic planning and risk evaluation. Examples are director, consultant, etc. Please refer to Table 1.1 for reference.

1.15.10   Define Systems Analysis and Design

Systems analysis is defined as a process of gathering and interpreting facts, diagnosing problems, and using the information to recommend improvements to the system. The systems design deals with how this improvement (generally in form of requirements) can be achieved. Systems analysis and design together is known as systems development.

1.15.11   Define Systems Analyst. Also List Duties of Systems Analyst in Organizations of Different Capacities

In a big organization, dedicated resources and experts are made available to perform various duties. A Systems Analyst has to perform analysis only. In medium firm, the duties of a Systems Analyst are to analyze and provide design of the system. In a small organization, the duties of Systems Analyst cover a big span. He has to do analysis, design, and programming.

1.15.12   What Systems Analysis Is Not for? What Is the Actual Purpose for Systems Analysis and Design?

Systems analysis is:

- Not for profit
- Not for computerization
- Not for the sake of change

However, the above changes are most likely to be observed while developing system. The basic objective of doing the systems analysis and design is to develop better procedures for business. Please refer Fig. 1.3.

1.15.13   List Three Approaches of Systems Analysis and Design

Systems Development Life Cycle (SDLC – also known as the classical approach), structured approach, and prototype are examples of major approaches to develop a system.

1.15.14 Give Full Form of SDLC and Describe Its Phases

The SDLC, which is also known as the classical model, is elaborated as Systems Development Life Cycle approach of developing a system. It is a sequential approach where predetermined steps need to be followed.

The phases of the SDLC are given as follows:

- Preliminary investigation: Deals with request clarification and operational, technical, and economical feasibility studies. If the systems development seems feasible, then request is approved.
- Determination of requirements: During this phase common and standard requirements are anticipated, new requirements are investigated through fact finding methods (interview, questionnaire, record review, and observation), and identified requirements are specified in terms of decision tree, decision table, and structured English.
- Design of system: Broad and detailed design, specifications, and layouts related to input, output, database, controls, runtime procedures, validation and verification, and test cases are designed in this phase.
- Development of system: According to the specified design, the systems modules are developed using third-generation programming languages such as C++ or Java or fourth-generation tools such as RDBMS packages. Computer Aided Systems Engineering (CASE) tools, .NET and other frameworks can also be utilized for the development of the system.
- Systems testing: Systems individual modules are tested (unit testing) and integrated. On the integrated system, again testing is carried out (integration testing). Some special systems tests such as peak load test, performance test, etc. are also carried out on the system.
- Implementation: The systems training is given to the target users if necessary, and old system is replaced with new system in direct, parallel, or phased manner.

Please refer to Fig. 1.4 for the SDLC model.

1.15.15 Explain Three Feasibility Tests for Systems Analysis and Design

The basic objective of feasibility test is to verify whether the proposed system is possible to develop and use.

There are three major feasibility tests, namely:

1. Economical feasibility
2. Technical feasibility
3. Operational feasibility

Economical Feasibility Refers to the ability of the system to offer economic benefits to the organization and its users against cost of development and cost of utilization of the system. Some times the cost of not developing system (that is what will be the cost and loss if we continue with the existing system) is also considered.

Technical Feasibility Verifies the availability and evaluation on technology, material/parts, equipment, personnel, and other logistics used during the development and use of the system. Quality aspects of the selected technology such as ease of use and friendliness, portability, security, flexibility, ability to store required volume of data, and other efficiency-oriented parameters can also be considered. Further, it is also needed to check whether the system developed with the selected technology can be enhanced in future or not (extendibility).

Operational Feasibility Checks the acceptability of the system by its target users (end users, managers, government, authority, suppliers, etc.) and ease of operation (use). The system must be useful and friendly to use and solves the users' problems. In any situation, the system must not produce unethical or harmful results.

1.15.16 Define and Explain the Brief Uses of Prototype Approach for Systems Analysis and Design

Prototype is defined as live, working model of the system. Before actual systems development, a working model of the system is developed in this approach in quick and iterative fashion. The uses of the prototype are given below:

- Prototype approach is used to collect additional requirements.
- Prototype is used to demonstrate expected features of the system and to test feasibility of the system.
- Prototype is used for development of novel and risky systems or system with the high cost.
- Prototype is used as a base model, which can be further revised to develop a full-fledged system.

1.15.17 What Are the Limitations of SDLC Model?

Limitations of the Systems Development Life Cycle (SDLC or classical model) are given below:

- SDLC is a sequential model. Once a phase is completed, you cannot go back. For example, once requirement determination phase is over, you cannot add/change the requirements.

- End user cannot see the solution till all the phases are completed. This will not allow solving a loss of translation problem (miscommunication via translating requirements of users). In this case users may not get what they want but a different solution.
- SDLC produces mass of documentation, at the end of each phase, which is required, but difficult to handle. Such documentation is costly and time taking.

1.15.18 Differentiate End User and Institutional Approach of Software Development

Table 1.9 Difference between institutional and end user approach

Institutional approach	End user approach
Institutional approach should be applied to the system that affects majority of an organization, such as payroll system	The candidate applications are limited in scope and producing output related to a department of an organization for its internal or temporary use
The responsibility of development is mainly on the Systems Analyst's and committee to develop system	The responsibility of development is mainly on the end users
Examples are tax planning system and attendance system	Examples are one-time query, reports of the existing system in different format, what-if analysis, etc.

1.15.19 What Are the Responsibilities of End Users in End User-Supported Systems Development Approach?

In the end user systems development approach, the responsibility to develop an application is in the hands of end user. The selected end users need to directly involve with all development phases, including requirement determination. The end users are supposed to do the following:

- End user must understand the business problem.
- End users often have to do the market survey for ready-made solutions and available tools.
- They should collect data limited to the business problem and prepare the data for further processing.
- They should have knowledge of user-friendly software packages which are suitable for the system. Systems Analyst can provide guidance to the end users in this process.
- End users also identify suitable quality standards, protocols, and metrics with the help of Systems Analyst.
- End users are responsible to develop and install system for use.
- End users are also responsible for necessary documentation, training, and conversion of the system.

1.15.20 List and Describe Various Information Systems Development Committees

Information Systems Group Responsibility of the development of system is solely on the information systems group under leadership of Systems Analyst.

Users Group Instead of information group or consultancy, end users are responsible to develop the system.

Consultancy/Outside Group Systems development responsibilities are on the shoulders of outside group.

Steering Committee Computer personnel (Systems Analyst, programmers, etc.); management personnel from various sections, especially skilled people (graphic designer, hardware engineer, etc.); and some users are involved to facilitate smooth development of the system.

1.15.21 List Broad Reasons for New Systems Development with Brief Description

Following are the broad reasons due to which new system needs to be developed:

- To solve a problem, if any reported/observed by users, authority, or Systems Analyst.
- To take advantage of opportunity and requirement in market, a new system is made or existing system is enhanced.
- To meet the demand by authority due to improved rules and regulations.

  Refer Table 1.3.

1.15.22 List Five Cs (Detailed Reasons) for New Systems Development with Brief Description

The following are the five Cs justifying the need of new systems development. These are also considered as objectives to develop new system as well as benefits expected from new system:

- Cost: To save the running and maintenance cost of the business
- Capacity: To increase the working capacity of the system
- Control: To improve the control on systems procedures for security, smooth operations, and better quality
- Communication: To enforce better communication between systems components

- Competitive Advantages: To take competitive advantages by maintaining users and keeping ahead of competitors

  Refer Table 1.4.

1.15.23 Define and Describe Portfolio

Systems portfolio in an organization is a collection of information systems which are in pipeline for development or currently being developed. When a proposal comes for a development of a system, it will undergo the request clarification, preliminary investigation, and feasibility analysis. After employing these activities, if the system seems to be worth for development, it will be included in the portfolio.

1.15.24 List Different Types of Portfolio Integrations with One-Line Description of Each

Each organization or a section with the organization should have at least one such portfolio. The portfolio facilitates the future view of the organization or section (the portfolio also provides facility to foresee near future of an organization). Different sections and organizations may share their respective portfolios for sharing their development views and mission.

Horizontal Organizations or sections at similar level (sister concerns) may join their portfolios to avoid duplication and share their development work.

Vertical Upper-level and lower-level organizations, apex bodies, and subdivisions of an organization, which can form a parent–children relationship, may use such vertical integration of portfolio. Here, subsystems can be developed at child (lower-level) organization and later integrated to build a bigger system.

Physical Portfolios with common background/domain from the physically remote locations can be integrated here.

External Some external systems related to the domain are integrated in the current portfolio. This is also done to utilize external data resources, techniques, and test libraries.

Refer Table 1.5 for detail.

1.15.25   Who Can Propose New Systems Development?

Development of a new system can be proposed by Systems Analyst, authority, end users, or any third party; however, it is considered for development after proper investigation and feasibility tests.

1.15.26   List Some Tools That Help in Systems Analysis and Design

During analysis, the emphasis is given to collect as many as facts related to the system. For the purpose, dictionary, charting, and data collection tools are helpful. Designing tools like UML, specification, and layout tools are helpful during the design phase. During development code generators, testing tools, and Computer-Aided Software/System Engineering (CASE) tools such as Rational Rose can be used.

1.16   Objective Questions

1.16.1   _____ is a set of components interacting together for common objectives and has common set of objectives.
    (a) Process   (c) Package
    (b) System   (d) Module

1.16.2   Open systems interacts with its environment for _____.
    (a) Demand   (c) Raw material
    (b) Feedback   (d) All of these

1.16.3   Closed system interacts with _____ while being used.
    (a) Environment   (c) Systems Analyst
    (b) Programmer   (d) Nothing

1.16.4   _____ are systems that work in structured environment for lower-level management using predefined rules in mechanical way.
    (a) Transaction Processing System   (c) Decision Support System
    (b) Management Information System   (d) Expert System

1.16.5   _____ is capable of not only providing decisions but also providing explanations and reasoning of the decisions taken by the system.
    (a) Transaction Processing System   (c) Decision Support System
    (b) Management Information System   (d) Expert System

1.16.6   Output of _____ type of systems is routine
and exceptional reports.
(a) Transaction   (c) Decision Support System
Processing System
(b) Management   (d) Expert System
Information System

1.16.7   A/An_____ works on knowledge base and database both.
(a) Transaction   (c) Decision Support System
Processing System
(b) Management   (d) Expert System
Information System

1.16.8   Example of logical boundary of system is _____.
(a) Time/Deadline   (c) Campus
(b) Wide area   (d) Town

1.16.9   _____ type of feedback is good but does not contribute much
besides appreciation and encouragement.
(a) Positive   (c) Adaptive
(b) Negative   (d) Corrective

1.16.10 Systems analysis deals with _____ are the problems with
the existing system, and systems
design deals with _____ it can be solved.
(a) When, how   (c) What, where
(b) How, what   (d) What, how

1.16.11 The basic goal of systems analysis and design focuses on _____.
(a) Changing interface   (c) Computerization
of the system
(b) Better quality procedures   (d) Profit

1.16.12 _____ type of users
performs the lower-level transactions.
(a) Hands on end users   (c) Admin
(b) Programmers   (d) Top-level managers

1.16.13 According to the well-known data pyramid
(DIKW hierarchy), data are _____
and information is _____.
(a) Processed, synthesized   (c) Pre-processed, processed
(b) Synthesized, processed   (d) Collected, pre-processed

1.16.14 _____ is a committee method to develop systems where
responsibility for project decision is delegated
to the individuals themselves.
(a) Contract-based development   (c) Steering committee
(b) Institutional   (d) End user

1.16.15 Which of the following is not a component of a typical system?
(a) Input   (c) Output
(b) Process   (d) Environment

1.16.16   _____ is an example of a typical Transaction
           Processing System (TPS).
           (a) Bank ATM system for   (c) Performance reports
                withdraw and deposit   of employee
           (b) Policy analysis   (d) All of these are TPS
1.16.17   _____ is an example of a Management
           Information System (MIS).
           (a) Performance reports   (c) Attendance system
                of employee
           (b) Disease diagnosing system   (d) Ticket reservation system
1.16.18   _____ is an example of a Decision Support System (DSS).
           (a) Student monitoring system   (c) Online shopping system
           (b) Maximization of production   (d) Robot controlling system
                and given constraints
1.16.19   _____ is a single information system that meets
           the needs of an organization at various levels and
           across many business functions.
           (a) Total information system   (c) Expert system
           (b) Decision support system   (d) None of these
1.16.20   Among which of the following system, _____ would
           be comparatively easy to automate?
           (a) DSS   (c) ES
           (b) MIS   (d) TPS
1.16.21   Which of the following is not an approach of developing
           an information system?
           (a) SDLC   (c) Structured
           (b) All of these are approaches   (d) Prototype
                of systems development
1.16.22   _____ test deals the acceptability of the system
           by its target users and ease of use.
           (a) Economical feasibility   (c) Operational feasibility
           (b) Technical feasibility   (d) Interface feasibility
1.16.23   _____ is also used as a feasibility tool.
           (a) SDLC   (c) Structured
           (b) Prototype   (d) None of these
1.16.24   _____ of development system is used for the development
           of system that considers systems that affect
           specific and limited group of users.
           (a) Institutional approach   (c) Prototype approach
           (b) End user approach   (d) Structured approach
1.16.25   _____ is an example of system that can be
           developed with an end user approach.
           (a) Sectional internal reports   (c) Attendance system
                and what-if analysis   for employees
           (b) Tax planning system   (d) ERP system

1.16.26 _____ is an example of analysis tools.
   (a) Specification   (c) Test case generator
   (b) Layout   (d) Dictionary
1.16.27 _____ is an example of design tools.
   (a) Specification   (c) Dictionary
   (b) Interview   (d) Questionnaire
1.16.28 _____ are integrated tools that can be used throughout
   systems analysis and design process.
   (a) Specification   (c) Test case generator
   (b) CASE   (d) Dictionary
1.16.29 _____ is a major limitation of the classical (SDLC) model
   of systems development.
   (a) Fixing requirements   (c) Effort taking approach
       at certain stage
   (b) Sequential approach   (d) None of these
       of the model
1.16.30 _____ approach of systems development is based
   on diagrams and charts.
   (a) SDLC   (c) Prototype
   (b) Structured   (d) None of these
1.16.31 _____ can suggest new systems development.
   (a) Managers   (c) Systems Analysts
   (b) End users   (d) All of these
1.16.32 Which of the following is not a broad objective of a new
   systems development?
   (a) To solve a problem   (c) To cut off number
                                            of employees
   (b) To computerize the business   (d) None of these
1.16.33 _____ is a collection of information system which
   is being developed or under development in an organization.
   (a) Electronic wallet   (c) Socket
   (b) Portfolio   (d) None of these
1.16.34 _____ integration of portfolio is defined as sharing
   portfolios within branches of an organization.
   (a) Horizontal   (c) External
   (b) Vertical   (d) Any of these
1.16.35 The _____ projects will not become part of a portfolio
   but must be reworked and proposed as a fresh project.
   (a) Feasible   (c) Special
   (b) Infeasible   (d) High cost

Answers

1.16.1	System	1.16.2	All of these
1.16.3	Nothing	1.16.4	Transaction Processing System
1.16.5	Expert System	1.16.6	Management Information System
1.16.7	Expert System	1.16.8	Time/Deadline
1.16.9	Positive	1.16.10	What, how
1.16.11	Better quality procedures	1.16.12	Hands on end users
1.16.13	Processed, synthesized	1.16.14	End user
1.16.15	Environment	1.16.16	Bank ATM system for withdraw and deposit
1.16.17	Performance reports of employee	1.16.18	Maximization of production and given constraints
1.16.19	Total information system	1.16.20	TPS
1.16.21	All of these are approaches of systems development	1.16.22	Operational feasibility
1.16.23	Prototype	1.16.24	End user approach
1.16.25	Sectional internal reports and what-if analysis	1.16.26	Dictionary
1.16.27	Specification	1.16.28	CASE
1.16.29	Fixing requirements at certain stage	1.16.30	Structured
1.16.31	All of these	1.16.32	To cut off number of employees
1.16.33	Portfolio	1.16.34	Horizontal
1.16.35	Infeasible		

References

Akerkar RA, Sajja PS (2009) Knowledge based systems. Jones & Bartlett Publishers, Sudbury
Senn JA (2008) Analysis and design of information systems. McGraw-Hill Education, New York

Chapter 2
Requirements Determination

Abstract Systems development encompasses systems analysis and systems design. Systems analysis is related with studying a system in depth to identify the limitations of the system and to discover features that can be added in order to improve the system. Such essential features are called requirements of the proposed system. Identification of good requirements and specifying them in an effective manner are essential activities during the systems development. Envisioning high-quality requirements leads to good-quality system. This chapter defines requirements determination process. The requirements anticipation, requirements investigation, and requirements specification are discussed thoroughly. The chapter also discusses requirements investigation in detail by providing discussion on fact-finding techniques such as interview, questionnaire, record review, observation, and prototyping. Decision tree, various types of decision tables, and structured English with its different forms are also discussed in this chapter. Many examples of the decision tree, table, and structured English are provided in this chapter. This chapter also discusses conversion of decision table into tree/structured English and vice versa with the help of real-life situations. The chapter provides various practice questions with answers at the end as well as objective questions with answers.

© Springer Nature Singapore Pte Ltd. 2017
P.S. Sajja, *Essence of Systems Analysis and Design*,
DOI 10.1007/978-981-10-5128-9_2

2.1   Introduction

Systems development is typically done in two phases, namely, systems analysis and systems design. During analysis of the system, the system is studied in depth to identify the limitations of the system and to discover "what" are the features or new facilities that can be added in the proposed system in order to improve the system. These essential features or facilities are known as requirements. Once good-quality requirements are finalized for a proposed system, the rough outline of the system is ready. At this stage, the new system is like a black box, as system is being analyzed and design is yet to be prepared. However, this black box gives you a rough idea about the behavior and output of the system. Determination of good requirements is the first step toward a good-quality system.

2.2   Phases of Requirements Determination

The requirements determination is carried out in three major phases, namely, (1) requirements anticipation, (2) requirements investigation, and (3) requirements specification. Table 2.1 enlists these phases with brief description of each phase.

Figure 2.1 illustrates these three phases.

Table 2.1 Phases of requirements determination

Phase	Description
Requirements anticipation	The obvious, standard, and common requirements are guessed by the Systems Analyst or developer based on his experience. For example, when an architect plans for a house, he generally plans for a kitchen; however, kitchen is not compulsory in every house. Anticipated requirements mainly yield common or biased products based on the developer's experience
Requirements investigation	The specific requirements must be properly investigated using the fact-finding methods (such as interview, questionnaire, record review, or observation) or prototyping. User preferences and domain-specific demands will be identified through proper investigation. For example, the architect will plan a kitchen at the ground floor in a house. If the user wants the kitchen at the first floor, this requirement must be communicated to him
Requirements specification	The anticipated or collected requirements must be specified in a well-formatted document. The document can further be used by the Analyst to communicate to the end user to give idea about the system, to the higher authority for the budget-related requirements, to the programmers for development, and to the testers to generate test cases and determine evaluation strategy
	The anticipated or investigated requirements are often listed in terms of decision tree, decision table, and structured English. Sometimes diagrams are also used. The systematic collection of requirements in above-specified form is often identified as "Software Requirements Specification (SRS)," which serves as an agreement between the developers, users, and managers

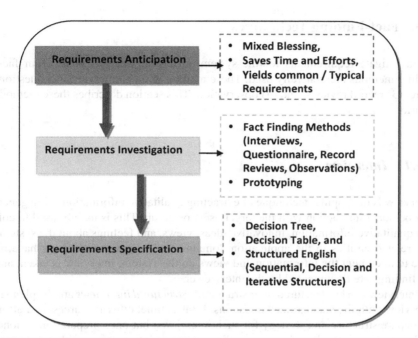

Fig. 2.1 Phases of requirements determination

The Software Requirements Specification (SRS) stating the determined requirements for the proposed system optionally contains the expected time to develop and expected outputs with a given resources as well as budget. Such SRS can be used as an agreement between the concerned parties. It may also contain about other conditions and constraints related to development of the systems, training of the system to the users, implementations and post implementation, and maintenance. The requirements listed in such SRS are often grouped into various categories such as functional, nonfunctional, quality, and security requirements (Pressman 2001 and Jalote 2005). SRS templates by IBM[1] and IEEE[2] are generally followed to document requirements in a formal way. Along with the abovementioned templates, examples and discussion are also available on the websites. However, it is to be noted that the requirements may not be always documented formally.

---

[1] https://www.ibm.com
[2] http://standards.ieee.org/

2.3   Fact-Finding Techniques

To investigate requirements for the system during the analysis phase, four fact-finding methods are generally used. These methods are (1) interview, (2) questionnaire, (3) record reviews, and (4) observation. This section describes these methods in brief.

2.3.1   Interview

Interview is the popular technique of extracting qualitative information using generally personal interaction with the target users or group. This is mainly used to collect qualitative information, innovative ideas, views, and feelings about the systems and related entities in the application domain. Also, when users/experts have no time to document the information and views on the system, interview is taken, and the findings are documented by the interviewer.

Interview can be structured or unstructured. *Structured interviews* are the planned interview with the standardized questions. It takes time, other resources, and effort to prepare structure and strategy for such interviews, but once preparation is done, such interviews can be taken in parallel by many interviewers with guaranteed uniformity. The structure of the interview generally contains the identified domains and sub-domains to be considered, timings, number of questions, quality of questions, and depth of the questions. The mechanism of documenting and evaluating the output is also decided prior to conducting the interview. Evaluation of result of the structured interview is also fast comparatively.

Unstructured Interviews provides free hands to the interviewers and users/experts. Here, the interviewer must be knowledgeable, free from any bias, and spontaneous as well. Such interview technique is more flexible and unstructured in nature. Here planning and preparation for the interview is negligible. On the other hand, it takes more effort and time to evaluate the results of such interviews. Further, the evaluation of such interviews by multiple evaluators may not be uniform.

2.3.2   Questionnaire

This method is used to collect quantitative information from a large number of people. One has to be very careful in the selection of questions and respondents in order to collect meaningful information. Questionnaire typically contains a set of written questions with or without choices. Once questionnaire is prepared, it can be send to many recipients simultaneously in offline or online manner. The questionnaire may contain closed-ended questions, where the user is not given much freedom to write their opinions, but has to select one option from the given options or give factual information such as production, year, population, and other quantitative data. Questionnaire may also contain open-ended questions in order to collect free-form answers and opinions (in a limited way) from its users.

With the questionnaire technique, information from many users can be collected simultaneously. Further, it is easy to automate and/or evaluate the information collected through questionnaire. Online questionnaires are also being popular nowadays. However, users are not given much freedom to express their feelings, as questionnaire is less flexible (however, less biased) in comparison with the interview technique.

2.3.3 Record Reviews

Documents, bills, receipts, invoices, reports, manuals, and correspondence belonging to the system within the organization often serve as useful resources to understand the working of the system and to collect requirements for the future system. Useful information, such as problem with existing systems, demands of the potential users, and problems with the existing system, can be identified with the record reviews. Record review can be a good source of information while designing the questionnaire and planning of interview as well as selecting target users.

2.3.4 Observation

All things cannot be well written in black and white. An Analyst must have capabilities to read between the lines and observe how the current system is working. Higher-level decisions are so tacit in nature; the procedure to take such decisions varies from person to person and hence cannot be documented. The observation technique helps Analyst to gather information which he cannot get through other fact-finding methods. For example, a manager cannot explain or interpret decision he has taken during business transactions in an interview. In this situation, observation technique is much useful. Observation technique will also be helpful in understanding the practical problems of users. For example, knowledge about how to conduct negotiations with suppliers and decisions to be taken at various organization levels can be learned with observation (and experience) only.

Besides these requirements investigation tools, many times other tools like prototype are used to collect requirements, especially when users cannot foresee the requirements. Here users are given demonstration of live working model (prototype) of the system, viewing which users may have an idea on how the proposed system actually works and provide insights about working of the proposed system. After that, users may provide additional requirements about their expectations, difficulties, and other requirements.

2.4   Tools for Documenting Procedures and Decisions

The acquired requirements need to be formally specified to facilitate communications to the managers, designers, programmers, and end users. The prominent tools for documenting the systems requirements are decision tree, decision table, and structured English. Most of these tools highlight conditions and suitable actions on the conditions involving the parameters on which decision has to be taken.

2.4.1   Decision Tree

As its name denotes, a decision tree is a kind of tree structure showing various conditions and actions in the form of roots, nodes, and branches. The root of a decision tree is a starting situation which occurs first in a sequence. One has to traverse from left to right starting from root or a given node representing action/further conditions. The general form of the decision tree (with two conditions) is shown in Fig. 2.2.

Consider an example of payment of fees in a school. If the fee is paid during the first 10 days of the month, then no penalty will be added to the fee amount. If fee is going to be paid after tenth of the month, then penalty of 100 dollars need to be paid extra. Decision tree for the situation is illustrated in Fig. 2.3.

Decision tree is easy to build and easy to follow. It identifies crucial decisions to be made and documents the decision-making processes in diagram form. The problem with the decision tree is its span over modules and sheets. It is tedious and infeasible to visualize and document all business decisions in a tree format, mainly because of its large number of branches and tedious process of forming the tree.

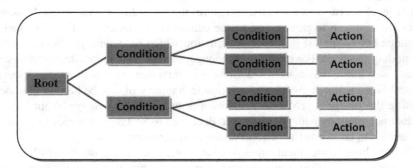

Fig. 2.2   Decision tree format

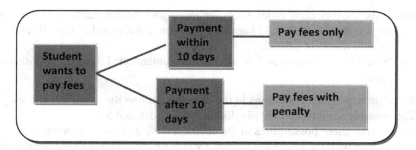

Fig. 2.3 Decision tree example

Table 2.2 General structure
of decision table

Condition	Action
Condition statements	Condition entries
Action statements	Action entries

2.4.2 Decision Table

Unlike decision tree, decisions and requirements are specified in the form of table. The decision table enlists possible situations and conditions along with necessary actions for each situation/condition. A decision table is a matrix encompassing condition statements, condition entries, action statements, and action entries. The general form of the decision table is given in Table 2.2.

Decision table is created by studying the number of conditions, their possible combinations of occurrences, and suitable actions to be taken. The first step is to identify all the possible conditions and combinations of the conditions in various situations. For each combination of the conditions, actions are determined. Once these condition entries and action entries along with their respective statements are determined, they are written in formal tabular format. The condition may involve one or more variables, which determines the size of the decision table.

Consider the example of online shopping of mobiles. If mobile order is within the first 5 days of the advertisement of the sale, 20% flat discount on the purchase is offered to the customers for orders of all sizes. After 5 days, 20% discount for orders above $ 10,000, 10% discount for orders between $ 5000 and $ 10,000, and 5% discount for orders below $ 5000 are offered. The simple decision table for this situation can be developed as follows:

1. Here two major factors affect the rate of discount, the order time and the order amount. These two factors are considered as decision variables. We may identify these two variables, respectively, as Time and Amount.
2. Write these two variables in the decision table as condition statements.
3. Let us identify all possibilities (combinations) of Time and Amount:

(a) In the case of early order, there are three possibilities, namely, (1) amount greater than $ 10,000, (2) amount between $ 5000 and $ 10,000, and (3) amount less than $ 5000.

(b) In case of subsequent orders, also the abovementioned three possibilities are there.

4. Write these possible conditions in the decision table as the condition entries.
5. The possible actions are to apply discount of 20, 10, and 5%.
6. Let us write these possibilities in the decision table as action statements.
7. Fill the gap with the necessary actions by putting cross marks in the appropriate cell of the table.

Table 2.3 Decision table example

Condition Statements	Condition Entries					
Time in days	<=5	<=5	<=5	>5	>5	>5
Amount in $	>=10k	5k to 10k	<5k	>=10k	5k to 10k	<5k
Action Statements	Action Entries					
20% discount	X	X	X	X		
10% discount					X	
5% discount						X

The decision table conditions must be checked before entering possible actions. There should not be duplication and redundancy in the statements and entries. If two or more combinations result in the same action, then the table can be simplified by combining these conditions.

It should be noted that with a single decision table, real-life complex decisions cannot be made. The decision table must support transfer of control from one decision table to another one. "Go to" and "Perform" are such control transfer statements that can be embedded into the decision table. The "Go to" facilitates the permanent transfer of control from one decision table to the specified one. In the case of "Perform," the control is temporarily transferred to the given decision table and returns after completing the decision job.

Forms of Decision Table The decision table varies by the way the condition alternatives and action entries are represented. The Table 2.3 illustrates a simple decision table. It can be mixed entry, extended entry, Yes/No entry, and else form.

In a limited entry form, the conditions are represented by simple Y (Yes) and N (No) and blank entries as shown in Table 2.4. The table illustrates the mobile and discount example in limited entry form.

In the extended entry from the conditions and actions are written verbally in descriptive form. Table 2.5 illustrates the mobile shopping and discount example in an extended entry form.

Table 2.4 Decision table: limited entry

Condition Statements	Condition Entries					
Within 5 days	Y	Y	Y	N	N	N
Over or equal to $ 10,000	Y			Y		
Between $ 5,000 to $ 9,999		Y			Y	
Less than $ 5,000			Y			Y
Action Statements	Action Entries					
20% discount	X	X	X	X		
10% discount					X	
5% discount						X

Table 2.5 Decision table: extended entry

Time in days	<=5	<=5	<=5	>5	>5	>5
Amount in $	>=10k	5k to 10k	<5k	>=10k	5k to 10k	<5k
	20% Disc.	20% Disc.	20% Disc.	20% Disc.		
Action					10% Disc.	
						5% Disc.

In the mixed entry form, the features of extended entry and limited entry decision tables are combined in one decision table. Table 2.3 presents an example of mixed entry form.

"Else" form of decision table combines all condition entries for which a common action has to be taken as shown in Table 2.6 which illustrates the mobile shopping and discount example in an "Else" form of decision table.

Decision table is a tool that not only manages and documents requirements but also facilitates encoding and testing of requirements. From the decision table, possible alternatives of various situations can be studied. Redundancy and contradiction in the decision table can be found out in easy way. Many programmers prefer decision table because of its structured nature. The policymakers, developers, and users all together can use decision table for understanding, communication, and development. Decision table often embedded with computer programs to automatically derive the underlying logic. Decision table processors are also available to provide partial automation and checking for redundancy and contradiction.

Table 2.6 Decision table: else form

Condition Statements	Condition Entries			
Time in days	>5	>5	>5	ELSE
Amount in $	>=10k	5k to 10k	- <5k	
Action Statements	Action Entries			
20% discount	X			X
10% discount		X		
5% discount			X	

2.4.3 Structured English

Requirements are often written in formal and structured way using structured English, instead of tree or table structure. Native English (or any language) is often ambiguous and cannot state conditions and actions clearly. Structured English with its predefined terminology offers advantages of English like representation. Instead of graphical representation, the structured English represents the decision-making process and underlying logic in narrative form using sequence structure, decision structure, and iteration structure. In sequence structure, sequential actions are listed in a specific order. The decision structure provides opportunity to take decision at a given stage. The iterative structure provides facility to document repetitive activities in systematic way. Figure 2.4 illustrates these structures with suitable examples.

Structured English can be written with general English keywords or with the help of pseudo language having predetermined number of keywords.

The structured English can be written using any pseudo language which is a subset of English language. It is relatively simple and does not involve any burden of showing the decision-making process graphically.

The above all structures (decision tree, decision table, and structured English) can be nested and used in conjunction with each other. That is, one can go for hybridization of these structures; for example, structured English and decision tables can be combined.

Table 2.7 compares the tools for documenting requirement against various parameters. For each parameter identified, comparative evaluation is specified.

As per Table 2.7 for developers such as designers, programmers, and testers, decision table is a preferred choice. Decision table has been the favorite topic of researchers too. However, research is going on in all the structures such as development of automatic cross-checking of decision table values, automatic compilation of code (in suitable programming language) from a given decision table, and development of new pseudo code language inherited from SGML family with specific tags such as <While>, <IF>, etc. while using the structured English.

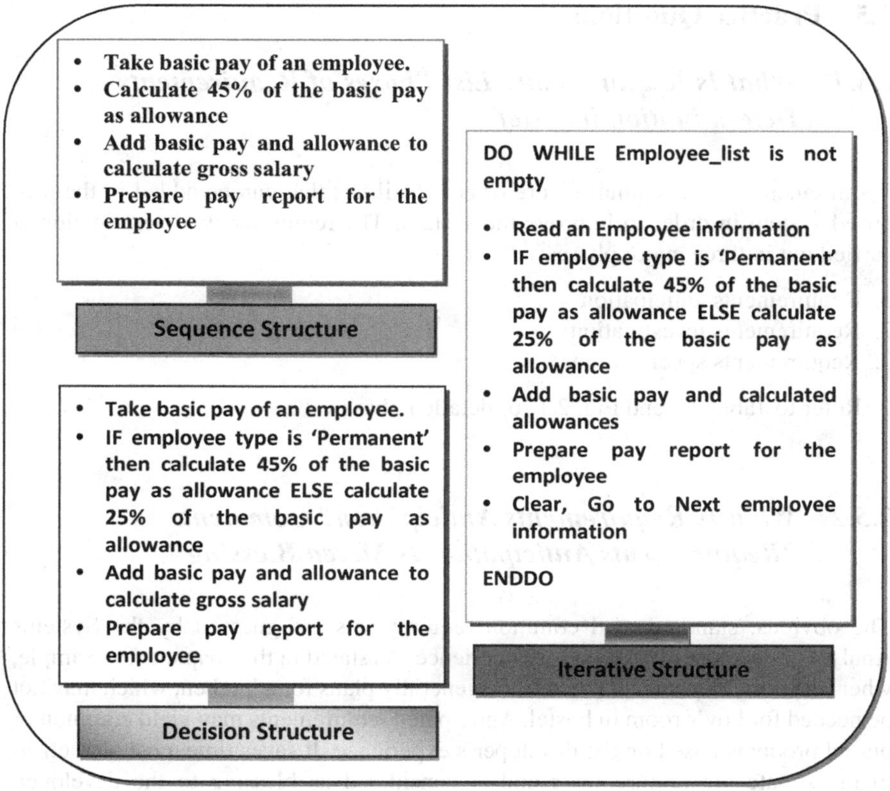

- Take basic pay of an employee.
- Calculate 45% of the basic pay as allowance
- Add basic pay and allowance to calculate gross salary
- Prepare pay report for the employee

Sequence Structure

- Take basic pay of an employee.
- IF employee type is 'Permanent' then calculate 45% of the basic pay as allowance ELSE calculate 25% of the basic pay as allowance
- Add basic pay and allowance to calculate gross salary
- Prepare pay report for the employee

Decision Structure

DO WHILE Employee_list is not empty

- Read an Employee information
- IF employee type is 'Permanent' then calculate 45% of the basic pay as allowance ELSE calculate 25% of the basic pay as allowance
- Add basic pay and calculated allowances
- Prepare pay report for the employee
- Clear, Go to Next employee information

ENDDO

Iterative Structure

Fig. 2.4   Structured English examples

Table 2.7   Comparison between decision tree, decision table, and structured English

Parameters	Decision tree	Decision table	Structured English
Readability (for end users)	Best	Good	Poor
Ease of development	Best	Poor	Good
Structuredness	Good	Best	Good
Visuality	Best	Good	Poor
Cross verification and evaluation	Poor	Best	Poor
Ability to encompass complicated logic	Poor	Best	Poor
Compactness	Poor	Best	Poor

2.5 Practice Questions

2.5.1 What Is Requirement? List Phases of Requirements Determination in Brief

Requirement is an essential feature or new facilities that can be added in the proposed system in order to improve the system. The requirements determination is carried out in three major phases:

1. Requirements anticipation
2. Requirements investigation
3. Requirements specification

Refer to Table 2.1 and Fig. 2.1 for detailed phases.

2.5.2 What Is Requirements Anticipation? Comment: "Requirements Anticipation Is Mixed Blessing"

The obvious, standard, and common requirements are guessed by the Systems Analyst or developer based on his experience. As stated in the chapter, for example, when an architect plans for a house, he generally plans for a kitchen, which may not be needed for boy's room in hostel. Anticipated requirements may yield common or biased products based on the developer's experience. It saves time, cost, and effort to investigate the requirements and is considered as blessing to the developer. However, it depends on the developer's experience and identifies typical requirements, thus generating a common product. This way it is a curse also. Here is the summary of the advantages and disadvantages of requirements anticipation:

Advantages

• It saves time, effort, and resources.
• Advantage of users' experience, knowledge, and insight will be provided to users with professional touch.

Disadvantages

• It results in stereotype, common, and typical product.
• The resulting product/outputs may be biased as per the experience and views of the developers.
• Some of the areas with new angle/recent development may be overlooked.

2.5.3 Define Fact-Finding Methods (List All Fact-Finding Methods with Its Objective and Short Description of Each Method)

The fact-finding methods are used to collect facts about the system under consideration. Facts about working of systems, users of system along with their roles and responsibilities, input and outputs of the system, etc. are collected for the purpose of analysis via fact-finding methods.

There are four fact-finding methods, namely, (1) interview, (2) questionnaire, (3) record reviews, and (4) observation.

During the systems analysis phase, via fact-finding methods, information about the system is collected. Emphasis is given on problems and issues of the system, along with future requirements. These methods are also used at end, after implementing and working with the delivered system to conduct post implementation analysis. Besides the abovementioned fact-finding methods, prototyping is also used as a tool to collect requirements from target users. Many times, the fact-finding methods, which procure advanced information and knowledge, are also known as knowledge acquisition.

Interview It is a way of direct interaction between the expert and the fact finder, here interviewer. It is the popular technique generally used to collect qualitative information, innovative ideas, views, and feelings about the systems and related entities in the application domain. It can be taken in face-to-face manner or using advanced technology such as telephonic/radio interview or video conferencing. Here the information provider need not have to document the information and views regarding the system; it is done by the interviewer.

Interview can be structured or unstructured. *Structured interviews* are the planned interview with the standardized questions. For the structured interviews, preparation and planning time is required. However, once preparation is done, such interviews can be taken in parallel by many interviews with guaranteed uniformity. For example, viva voce (oral exam) of students can be taken in parallel by many teachers with standardized questions in specified time limit per student. Evaluation of the result of the structured interview is also fast comparatively. *Unstructured interview*, on the other hand, provides free hands to the interviewers and users. Here, the interviewer must be knowledgeable, spontaneous, and free from any bias. Such interview technique is more flexible and hence unstructured in nature. Here planning and preparation for the interview is not necessary. On the other hand, it takes more effort and time to evaluate the results of such interviews.

Questionnaire It is used to collect quantitative information from a large number of people in online or offline manner. Questionnaire typically contains a set of written questions with or without choices. The questionnaire may contain closed-ended questions, where the user is not given much freedom to write their opinions, but has to select one option from the given options or give factual information such as production, year, population, and other quantitative data. With the questionnaire technique, information from many users can be collected simultaneously. Further, it is easy to automate and/or evaluate the information collected through questionnaire. If online questionnaire is used, data are collected from multiple users in very efficient manner. Further evaluation and presentation of such collected data are also very easy. However, in the case of questionnaire, users are not given much freedom to express their feelings, as questionnaire is less flexible (but standard and less biased) in comparison with the interview technique.

Record Reviews The organization documents, bills, receipts, invoices, reports, manuals, and correspondence often serve as useful resources to understand the working of the system and to collect requirements for the future system. Useful information, such as problem with existing systems, demands of the potential users, and problems with the existing system, can be identified with the record reviews. Record review can be a good source of information while planning for questionnaire and interview questions and selecting target users to interview and send questionnaire.

Observation All things are not written in black and white. An Analyst must have capabilities to read between the lines and observe the current system working. Higher-level decisions are so tacit in nature; the procedure to take such decisions varies person to person and hence cannot be documented. The observation technique helps Analyst to gather information which he cannot get through other fact-finding methods. For example, a manager cannot explain or interpret decision he has taken in an interview. In this situation, observation technique is much useful. Observation technique will also be helpful in understanding the practical problems of users. For example, knowledge about how to do negotiations with suppliers can be obtained with observation only.

Besides these fact-finding methods, prototype (live working model of the system) can also be used to collect information related to systems from users. This is generally used when users are not aware of systems (or technology's) working, system is innovative in one or more ways, or it is risky (in terms of time, cost, and effort involved) to develop system without considering users' feedback and support.

2.5.4 When Technique of Observation Is Used to Collect Facts Related to the System?

Please refer to answer of Question 2.5.3.

Table 2.8 Difference between structured and unstructured interview

Structured interview	Unstructured interview
Well-planned framework of interview in terms of questions and time, and hence similar questions are considered with equal time	No such framework, no guarantee of consistency (similar questions to different candidates) and time. It saves time of training the interviewers
Preparation time and planning is required	Planning and preparation is not needed
Evaluation is easy	Evaluation is difficult because of unstructuredness of the content extracted in various interview sessions
Interviewer needs to follow the framework; there is no opportunity to be dynamic and spontaneous	Interviewer can be dynamic and spontaneous

2.5.5 Besides Typical Fact-Finding Methods, Which Other Techniques Can Be Used to Collect Facts Related to the System?

It is prototype. Prototype is used as requirements elicitation tools, feasibility testing tools, and iterative development approach to develop information system. Please refer to answer of Question 2.5.3.

2.5.6 Distinguish Between Structured and Unstructured Interview

Difference between structured and unstructured interview is given as follows (Table 2.8).

2.5.7 What Is Closed-Ended Questionnaire? Give an Example

Closed-ended questionnaire contains questions for which the user is not given much freedom to write their opinions, but has to select one option from the given options or give factual information such as production, year, population, and other quantitative data, e.g., "What is the production (in metric ton) of the chocolate factory, Mumbai branch, in the year 2016?" To respond to this question, a user has to give a figure only. This is an example of the closed-ended questionnaire. Another example is: "Are you satisfied with the performance of your teacher? Say Yes/No" is a query in a survey while taking feedback of the teacher about a course. Students merely have to say either "Yes" or "No." Reasons regarding the issue can be taken in open-ended questionnaires.

2.5.8   List Any Two Tools for Documenting the Requirements, with Brief Description of Each

The prominent tools for documenting the systems requirements are decision tree, decision table, and structured English. A brief description on decision tree and decision table is given below:

Decision Tree Decision tree is a kind of tree structure showing various conditions and actions in the form of roots, nodes, and branches. The root of a decision tree is a starting action which occurs first in a sequence. One has to traverse from left to right starting from root or a given node representing an action. Please refer to Figs. 2.2 and 2.3.

Decision tree is easy to build and easy to follow. It identifies crucial decisions to be made and documents the decision-making processes in diagram form. The problem with the decision tree is its span over modules and sheets. It is tedious and infeasible to visualize and document all business decisions in a tree format, mainly because of its large number of branches and tedious process of forming the tree.

Decision Table A decision table is a matrix encompassing condition statements, condition entries, action statements, and action entries. Decision table is created by studying the number of conditions, their possible combinations of occurrences, and suitable actions to be taken. The first step is to identify all the possible conditions and combinations of the conditions in various situations. For each combination of the conditions, actions are determined. Once these condition entries and action entries are determined, they are written in a formal tabular format. The condition may involve one or more variables, which determines the size of the decision table. Please refer to Table 2.2 for the general form of decision tree, and refer to Tables 2.3, 2.4, 2.5, and 2.6 for examples of decision table.

The decision table must be checked for duplication and redundancy. The "Go to" and "Perform" are used for permanent and temporary transfer of control between decision tables.

There are mixed entry, Yes/No entries, extended entry, and else entry forms available for decision table. Please refer to Sect. 2.4.2 for decision table-related details.

2.5.9   List Characteristics of Decision Tree (Also Give General Form of the Decision Tree)

A decision tree is a kind of tree structure having root and nodes of the tree as conditions and actions. It is a diagram that shows conations and actions in a tree form. The root of a decision tree is a starting action which occurs first in a sequence. One has to traverse from left to right starting from root or a given node representing action. The general form of the decision tree is shown at Fig. 2.2.

The characteristics of the decision tree are as given below:

- A decision tree is easy to build and easy to follow. No specific training is required to understand the tree.
- It identifies crucial decisions to be made and documents the decision-making processes in diagram form.

A decision tree documents business decisions in form of a tree. Because of large number of branches and tedious process of forming the tree, it makes the tree creation process difficult for real-life businesses.

2.5.10 What Are the Components of a Decision Table? Also List Different Types/Formats of Decision Table

A decision table is a matrix encompassing condition statements, condition entries, action statements, and action entries. The general form of the decision table is given at Table 2.2.

There are mixed entry, Yes/No entries, extended entry, and else entry forms available for decision table.

2.5.11 What Are the Benefits Formally Specifying Requirements? Or What Are the Benefits of the Formal Software Requirements Specification (SRS)?

Formal specification of requirements (or SRS document) serves as an agreement between the users and developers for the system being developed. Here are the advantages of requirements specifications to different stakeholders:

- *To end users*: Formal specification of requirements helps in understanding the system that will be delivered to them at the end.
- *To developers*: It is easy to accommodate requirements while development. Further, it is also easy to cross verify given requirements at every phase of development through formal specification. Total time, effort, and cost for development can also be estimated from the requirements specified.
- *To programmers*: Formally presented requirements help programmers to develop code as per the requirements.
- *To testers*: Formal specification of requirements also helps in development of appropriate test cases checking the necessary requirements and to test given software or systems procedures.
- *To managers*: It is convenient for authority and managers to arrange necessary resources and plan activities as the requirements for development and after development if the requirements are known in advance. From SRS time, effort, and resources (such as manpower/programmers, hardware and software, etc.) to develop system can be planned in advance.

Table 2.9 Decision table for tax calculation

Condition statements	Condition entries					
Tax paid before October 31	Y	Y	Y	N	N	N
Annual salary above $ 1,000,000	Y			Y		
Between $ 500,000 and $ 1,000,000		Y			Y	
Less than $ 500,000			Y			Y
Action statements	**Action entries**					
30% Tax	X			X		
20% Tax		X			X	
10% Tax			X			X
Late fees 2% extra tax				X	X	X

Table 2.10 Decision table for tax calculation: an alternative way

Condition statements	Condition entries					
Tax paid before October 31	Y	Y	Y	N	N	N
Annual salary above $ 1,000,000	Y			Y		
Between $ 500,000 to $ 1,000,000		Y			Y	
Less than $ 500,000			Y			Y
Action statements	**Action entries**					
30% Tax	X					
20% Tax		X				
10% Tax			X			
30% Tax +2% late fee				X		
20% Tax +2% late fee					X	
10% Tax +2% late fee						X

2.5.12 Give an Example of a Decision Table

Consider an example of the income tax calculation for an employee of an organization. Consider rules to calculate income tax as follows.

If the annual taxable income of an employee is less than $ 500,000, then the tax is 10% of the taxable income. If the annual taxable income of an employee is between $ 500,000 and $ 1,000,000, then the tax is 20% of the taxable income. In other cases, the tax is 30% of the taxable income. If the tax is not paid till 31st of October, then the late fee of 2% on the taxable income is to be paid besides the tax. The decision table for the example is given below (Table 2.9).

Alternatively, the same table can also be written as follows (Table 2.10).

2.5.13 How Control Can Be Transferred in a Decision Table?

"Go to" and "Perform" are the control transfer statements that can be embedded into the decision table. The "Go to" facilitates the permanent transfer of control from one decision table to the specified one. In the case of "Perform," the control is temporarily transferred to the given decision table and returns after completing the decision job.

2.5.14 Convert the Decision Table Given at Table 2.3 into Its Equivalent Decision Tree (Fig. 2.5)

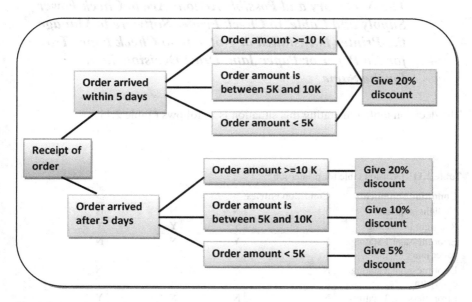

Fig. 2.5 Decision tree for book order

2.5.15 Convert the Decision Table Given at Table 2.3 into Its Equivalent Structured English

IF (mobile order arrival time) <= 5 days
   Give 20% discount;
ELSE IF (order arrival time) >5 days AND (order amount) >= 10K
   Give 20% discount;
ELSE IF (order arrival time) >5 days AND (5K<=(order amount) <10K)
   Give 10% discount;
ELSE IF (order arrival time) >5 days AND (order amount) <5K)
   Give 10% discount;

2.5.16 Consider a Situation of Printing Document Using Printer Attached with a Desktop Computer. Printer Job Is Not Successfully Carried Out Because of Many Conditions such as the Following: There Is No Paper in the Tray, Printer Is Not Installed or Not Recognized by the Machine, or Printer Shows Error (Red Light). The Necessary and Possible Actions Are to Check Power Supply and Cable, to Check Proper Software to Manage the Printer Is Installed or Not, and to Check Paper Tray for No Paper or Paper Jam. Draw Decision Table for the Same

The decision table illustrating this situation is as follows (Table 2.11).

Table 2.11 Decision table for printer job

Condition statements	Condition entries			
No light on printer	Y	N	N	N
Red light is flashing	N	Y	Y	Y
Error message 1 stating paper jam	N	Y	N	N
Error message 2 stating empty tray	N	N	Y	N
Error message 3 stating printer not recognized	N	N	N	Y
Action statements	**Action entries**			
Action 1	Check power supply and printer cable			
Action 2		Clear printer tray		
Action 3			Add papers in printer tray	
Action 4				Install proper printer software

2.5.17   Consider Online Shopping Scenario. Typically When a Big Order Is Given, the Customer Is Given Handsome Discount. In Case of Some Selected Products, "Cash on Delivery" Option Is Also Available. The Delivery Charges Are Applicable to Some of the Product. Consider the Following Products Along with Information About Their Discounts, Delivery Charges, and Facilities Such as "Cash on Delivery"

- First Product: Product code is 1, and product category name is Grocery.

  - If more than 50 units are ordered, then 10% discount on product price is provided.
  - Cash on delivery is available.
  - No delivery charge is applicable.

- Second Product: Product code is 2, and product category name is Major_Electronic.

  - If more than 50 units are ordered, then 10% discount on product price is provided.
  - Cash on delivery is not available.
  - Delivery charge is $ 100 per unit.

Table 2.12   Decision table for online shopping

Condition statements	Condition entries			
Product	Product code 1		Product code 2	
	Product category Grocery		Product category Major-Electronic	
Order <50 units	Y	N	Y	N
Order > = 50 units	N	Y	N	Y
Cash on delivery	Y	Y	N	N
Action statements	**Action entries**			
Discount 10%		X		X
Delivery charges $ 100 per unit			X	X
Free delivery	X	X		

2.5.18   Consider Typical Software Developed for Routine Office Procedures Requiring Authentication of the User via "Sign In" Facility Through Username and Password. The Password Recovery Mechanism Is Also Embedded Using the "Forget Password" Mechanism for the Users

Generate a decision table to demonstrate the situation as well as to be used as a test case for checking proper authentication of the user.

Table 2.13   Decision table for users' authentication

Condition statements	Condition entries					
Username provided	Yes	Yes	No	Yes	No	No
Password provided	Yes	No	Yes	No	No	No
Forget password request	No	No	No	Yes	Yes	No
Action statements	**Action entries**					
Login successful	Yes	–	–	–	–	–
Login denied	–	Yes	Yes	–	–	–
Mail new password to registered mail address	–	–	–	Yes	–	–
Ask for sign up procedure	–	–	–	–	Yes	Yes

2.5.19   Explain Three Forms of Structured English with Example of Each

There are three forms of the structured English: (1) sequence structure, (2) decision structure, and (3) iteration structure.

Sequence Structure   Represents every process or phases in sequential manner.

Example

- Take student's identification number and other information.
- Collect six subject marks for the student.
- Calculate total and percentages of the student.
- Prepare information sheet for a student containing student identification number, name, other information, and marks with total and percentages.

Decision Structure   It is used to represent two or more actions, one of which is to be executed depending on value of a decision variable.

Example

- Take student's identification number and other information.
- Collect six subject marks for the student.
- Calculate total and percentages of the student.
- IF percentage of student is greater than 40%, then set result equal to "Pass" ELSE "Fail."

- Prepare information sheet for a student containing student identification number, name, other information, and marks with total and percentages.
- Also print result as "Pass" or "Fail."

Iteration Structure It provides facility to document repetitive activities in systematic way.

Example
DO WHILE Students _list is not empty

- Take student's identification number and other information.
- Collect six subject marks for the student.
- Calculate total and percentages of the student.
- IF percentage of student is greater than 40%, then set result equal to "Pass" ELSE "Fail."
- Prepare information sheet for a student containing student identification number, name, other information, and marks with total and percentages.
- Also print result as "Pass" or "Fail."
- Clear and go to next student's information.

ENDDO

2.5.20 Convert the Decision Table Given at Exercise Question 2.5.18 (About "Sign In" and "Forget Password Utility") of This Chapter into Its Equivalent Decision Tree

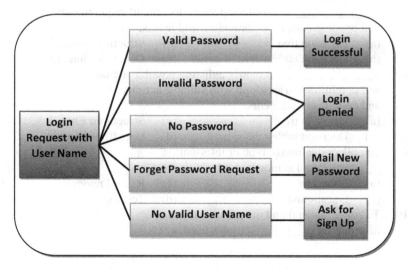

Fig. 2.6 Decision tree for users' authentication

2.6   Objective Questions

2.6.1 _____ is a feature that must be added into the system
to improve quality of the system.
   (a)   Requirement   (c)   Code
   (b)   Computer   (d)   All of these

2.6.2 Good requirements often lead to _____ system, but bad
requirements always lead to the _____.
   (a)   Good, bad   (c)   Good or bad, bad
   (b)   Bad, good   (d)   Any of these

2.6.3 Determination of _____ is the first step toward
a good-quality system.
   (a)   Good requirements   (c)   Good infrastructure
   (b)   Good programmers   (d)   Good protocols

2.6.4 _____ is a phase of requirements determination.
   (a)   Requirements anticipation   (c)   Requirements specification
   (b)   Requirements determination   (d)   All of these

2.6.5 Requirements _____ is a mixed blessing.
   (a)   Anticipation   (c)   Specification
   (b)   Investigation   (d)   Determination

2.6.6 _____ are used for requirements investigation.
   (a)   Validation methods   (c)   Fact-finding methods
   (b)   Decision tree-based   (d)   Testing methods
        methods

2.6.7 _____ is a tool to specify (document) requirements
that encompasses roots, branches, and leaves.
   (a)   Decision tree   (c)   Structured English
   (b)   Decision table   (d)   Data flow diagram

2.6.8 _____ is a matrix enlisting possible action
and condition entries along with suitable actions
and condition statements.
   (a)   Decision tree   (c)   Structured English
   (b)   Decision table   (d)   Data flow diagram

2.6.9 To collect qualitative type of information
_____ tool is mostly used.
   (a)   Interview   (c)   Record review
   (b)   Questionnaire   (d)   Testing

2.6.10 To collect factual and quantitative type of
information _____ tool is used.

    (a)   Interview   (c)   Record review

    (b)   Questionnaire   (d)   Observation

2.6.11 For _____ interview, training and preparation is not needed.

    (a)   Unstructured   (c)   Exceptional

    (b)   Structured   (d)   Big

2.6.12 For _____ interview, evaluation is speedy and uniform.

    (a)   Unstructured   (c)   Exceptional

    (b)   Structured   (d)   Big

2.6.13 For _____ questionnaire short and limited scope answers are expected.

    (a)   Open end   (c)   Closed end

    (b)   Domain specific   (d)   Online

2.6.14 For _____ questionnaire big answers can be expected.

    (a)   Open end   (c)   Closed end

    (b)   Domain specific   (d)   Online

2.6.15 _____ is also used as requirements finding and feasibility testing tool.

    (a)   Prototype   (c)   System

    (b)   Reports   (d)   Procedure

2.6.16 For _____ requirements, requirements anticipation is suitable.

    (a)   Extraordinary   (c)   Big

    (b)   Common and typical   (d)   Complex

2.6.17 Requirements investigation utilizes _____ methods.

    (a)   Fact finding   (c)   Both fact finding and prototype

    (b)   Prototype   (d)   Testing

2.6.18 An SRS (documents the determined requirements for the proposed system) is defined as _____.

    (a)   Simple reliable software   (c)   Software reusable simplicity

    (b)   Systematic requirements specification   (d)   Software Requirements Specification

2.6.19 _____ contains valid set of requirements documented in well-organized form and serves as an agreement between the developers and users of the system.

    (a)   SRS   (c)   User manual

    (b)   Documentation   (d)   Project

2.6.20 An SRS includes _____.

    (a)   Valid requirements   (c)   Tentative cost to develop the project

    (b)   Estimated time   (d)   All of these

2.6.21   Higher-level decisions in the development of system, which
         are tacit in nature, cannot be put into words. Such requirements
         can be identified through _____ fact-finding method.
         (a)   Viewing records   (c)   Observation
         (b)   Feasibility analysis   (d)   Documentation

2.6.22   _____ are the tools for documenting systems requirements.
         (a)   Decision tree   (c)   Decision table
         (b)   Structured English   (d)   All of these

2.6.23   _____ control in a decision table allows temporary
         control transfer between decision tables.
         (a)   Perform   (c)   Return
         (b)   Go to   (d)   Execute

2.6.24   _____ control in a decision table allows permanent
         control transfer between decision tables.
         (a)   Perform   (c)   Return
         (b)   Go to   (d)   Execute

2.6.25   _____ are valid representations schemes in structured English.
         (a)   Sequence structure   (c)   Iteration structure
         (b)   Decision structure   (d)   All of these

Answers

2.6.1	Requirement	2.6.2	Good or bad, bad
2.6.3	Good requirements	2.6.4	All of these
2.6.5	Anticipation	2.6.6	Fact-finding methods
2.6.7	Decision tree	2.6.8	Decision table
2.6.9	Interview	2.6.10	Questionnaire
2.6.11	Unstructured	2.6.12	Structured
2.6.13	Closed end	2.6.14	Open end
2.6.15	Prototype	2.6.16	Common and typical
2.6.17	Both fact finding and prototype	2.6.18	Software Requirements Specification
2.6.19	SRS	2.6.20	All of these
2.6.21	Observation	2.6.22	All of these
2.6.23	Perform	2.6.24	Go to
2.6.25	All of these		

References

Jalote P (2005) An integrated approach to software engineering. Springer Science & Business Media, New York

Pressman RS (2001) Software engineering: a practioner's approach. McGraw-Hill Higher Education, New York

Chapter 3
Structured Systems Development Approach

Abstract This chapter discusses structured systems development approach. The chapter defines the structured systems development approach and establishes the need of the approach. The chapter discusses with many illustrations the function hierarchy charts and data flow diagram (DFD). Notations and examples of data flow diagrams are well presented in this chapter. To name a few, context-level and detailed-level data flow diagrams are discussed for product inventory, student attendance, bank ATM transactions, library management systems, and outdoor hospital management systems. The chapter also discusses notion of physical and logical data flow diagrams. The importance and usage of such data flow diagrams are also discussed. Many times users do some common mistakes while developing data flow diagrams. These mistakes are discussed in depth with necessary examples as well as many graphical illustrations representing different situations. Further, the chapter discusses concept of data dictionary by considering its use, its components, and its advantages. At the end, the chapter discusses the function-oriented approach and object-oriented approach by taking a common system and providing design hints in both the ways. The practice questions at the end consider various real-life situations and present data flow diagram for the same, besides concept-based questions and answers. In some of the examples, invalid data flow diagram (diagram with false data) is provided with required corrections. Objective questions are also provided in this chapter with answers.

© Springer Nature Singapore Pte Ltd. 2017
P.S. Sajja, *Essence of Systems Analysis and Design*,
DOI 10.1007/978-981-10-5128-9_3

3.1 Structured Development Approach

Many real-life systems are complex and big. These two characteristics of a system make the development of the system difficult. It would be easy if the system is partitioned into some modules and then taken into consideration for development. Each component of a system is developed with ease and control because of its reduced size and complexity. Once all the modules are developed, they are combined for an integrated solution. Such divide and conquer technique is very organized and structured, hence called structured development technique. Another advantage of the structured development approach is the ability to work in parallel. Once system is divided into components, they can be considered for further development in parallel. Work of Yourdon and Larry (1979) and Gane and Sarson (1977) are the key instruments in utilizing such modular approach into reality.

The structured development approach includes structured analysis and structured design. Structured analysis focuses on identifying facts of the system and limitations of the system in order to find out new systems requirements. It focuses on "what" are the features and facilities that the new system should provide to overcome limitations of the existing system. Since the analysis is carried out in structured manner, it follows modular approach. This helps in parallel analysis of different modules by many analysts with commonly set objectives. Structured design focuses on "how" to meet these limitations and implements solutions of these identified limitations of the system. Here also modular approach is followed.

Structured development depends on graphic description. To study the existing systems working and to demonstrate new systems model and design, diagrams like function decomposition diagram, data flow diagrams, and Unified Modeling Language (UML)-based diagrams are used. Other important components include data dictionary, rules and procedure, and process description.

3.2 Function Hierarchy Charts

A function hierarchy chart shows decomposition of system into modules using a treelike structure. It is a kind of top-down design that considers system as its root level and breaks down the system into modules. The modules are further divided into sub-modules. It generally specifies high-level design of the system; hence, it is called high-level design or systems design. Since it decomposes the system into possible modules, it is also known as function decomposition diagram (FDD). Such diagram can show size and complexity of the system, number of modules in it, and coupling (relationship) between the modules in hierarchical fashion. The system should be decomposed in such a way that most of its modules have minimal dependency (coupling) on each other. Figure 3.1 shows a general structure of a function decomposition diagram (FDD).

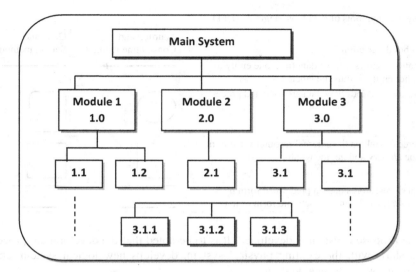

Fig. 3.1 Function decomposition diagram (FDD) structure

Since the modules are coming from a common/parent (system), their interdependencies cannot be reduced to null. However, these modules must be as independent as possible to avoid development and usage difficulties. In similar manner, the internal logic and relationship (bond) between components of a module must be strong. Such internal strength of a module is known as cohesion. The cohesion is desired to be maximum (as high as possible), and coupling is desired to be minimum (as low as possible). Number of modules divided from the parent module should also be reasonable and should not be too many or too less.

3.3   Data Flow Diagrams

To understand the existing system, it is mandatory to understand the dataflow between components of the business/system. Which data are used, who uses these data, what data are entered, and what data is outgoing from the system must be known to understand the existing system and to design a new solution. The dataflow can be shown pictorially to understand, to demonstrate, and to communicate the working of a system. Such diagram is known as a data flow diagram (DFD). DFDs model systems working by showing how input data is transformed to output results through a sequence of functional transformations. At initial point of systems development, the DFD is generally made to understand the existing physical system. After thorough study of the system, a logical systems model is developed on paper and analyzed covering limitations of the existing system. This is the conceptual design of the new system. Based on the conceptual design, a physical design (DFD)

Table 3.1 Symbols of data flow diagrams (DFD)

Symbol description	Yourdon and Constantine method	Gane and Sarson method
Dataflow: shows flow of data from one entity to another entity. It must be labeled	⟶	⟶
Process: describes how data are used and processed	◯	▢
Source or sink: is the external resources that initiate request/query and get the results	▢	▢
Data stores: stores data in predefined form by a process. It can be in an electronic form or not	▭	▭

of the proposed system is developed. It is to be noted that the development procedure starts with the existing physical system, develops new logical system, and
completes with physical systems.

3.3.1 DFD Notations

DFDs consist of four major components: entities, processes, data stores, and dataflows. There are two notation schemes for the same: Yourdon and Constantine
(1979) and Gane and Sarson (1977) representation. These notations are illustrated
in Table 3.1.

3.3.2 Examples of the Data Flow Diagrams (DFDs)

Consider a typical inventory of ice-cream factory. The inventory manages the finished and semifinished products in it. On valid demand, the inventory provides
information in proper format and product to the users. In case the inventory is not
capable of providing the material or information to the user, it will acknowledge the
same. The inventory will also receive query for information, products, and user
information.

Let us divide the inventory management system into three basic functions,
namely, (1) login or reception (for manual system), (2) transactions such as adding
material to the inventory and issuing material from the inventory, and (3) the information required to be provided into report format. According to this main information, a function decomposition diagram (FDD) is prepared as shown in Fig. 3.2.

On requirement, the modules shown in Fig. 3.2 can be further expanded allowing
minimum dependency on each other and maximum tightness (bond) within them.
These concepts, as stated earlier, are known as coupling and cohesion,
respectively.

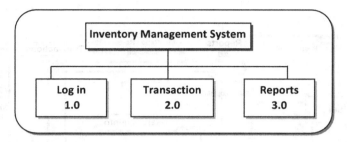

Fig. 3.2 Function decomposition diagram (FDD)

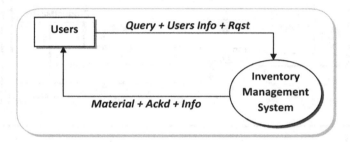

Fig. 3.3 Context-level DFD of the inventory example

The function decomposition diagram (FDD) outlines the data flow diagram (DFD) design. According to FDD modules, processes of the DFD can be designed. Figure 3.2 describes two levels of hierarchy, among which the first level is identified as root level. For every level of the FDD, One or more DFD can be drawn. At root level a context (bird's eye view of the system) diagram is drawn. Figure 3.3 provides a context-level DFD for the example of the inventory management system in accordance with the FDD shown in Fig. 3.2.

The context-level diagram shows all possible inputs and outputs with the system with external entities and resources. In Fig. 3.3, users are playing role of source or external entity. Users can make request for login (Rqst), provide user information (Users Info) for first time sign up and then sign in procedures, and query (Query) for information from the system. These inputs may not be given at a time in a single cycle but in different point of time and on requirement. The system may provide output such as acknowledgment (Ackd) of the request, information (Info), and requested material (Material).

The lower-level DFDs must match with the context-level DFD. Figure 3.4 illustrates the immediate-level (next to context-level) DFD of the inventory management system. The diagram shown in Fig. 3.4 is developed using Microsoft Viso[1] tool.

On requirement, the DFD shown in Fig. 3.4 can further be expanded as per the modules designed in the corresponding FDD of the system.

---

[1] https://products.office.com/en-in/visio/flowchart-software

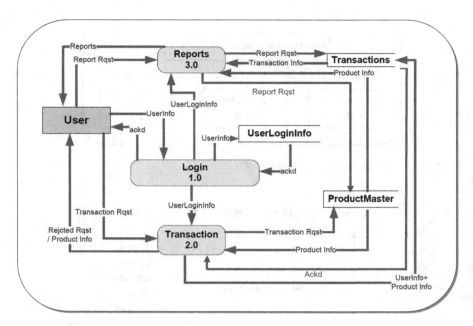

Fig. 3.4 Immediate-level DFD for the inventory example

3.3.3   Physical and Logical DFDs

Physical DFD is the implementation-dependent view of the current system. It encompasses people, tasks, and location information. Also it may include names of forms, documents, departments, equipment, devices, related procedures, etc. As it contains physical information regarding the system, it is called physical DFD.

Logical DFD is an implantation-independent view of the current system. It focuses on the flow of data between processes and other entities. It does not give importance to the physical entities of the system but focuses on logical (conceptual) working of the system. They are more abstract (in comparison with the physical DFDs) and help a lot in analyzing the system.

The DFDs whether physical or logical should not contain time or control information; for this purpose flowcharts are useful.

3.3.4   Uses of the FDDs and DFDs

DFDs and FDDs are helpful in many ways. Some of the uses are listed below:

- To understand (analyze) working of the given system
- To demonstrate design of new system
- To communicate the design to the users and developers

- To discuss and review the design of the proposed system
- To isolate areas for better focusing, as DFDs and FDDs follow a hierarchical representation
- To cross verify the outputs at the end to satisfy the users' demand while testing
- To document the design for future use

DFDs are simple and hierarchical and have visual appeal to its users. Further, it uses top-down approach of representing a systems design. Since it uses only a few symbols, it is easy for most of the people to read them.

3.3.5   Common Mistakes While Developing FDDs and DFDs

Most of the FDDs and DFDs are readable and simple because the meaningful names along with a limited number of symbols are used. However, often developers do some mistakes. Some common mistakes are summarized as follows:

- Forgetting label on any entity, especially forgetting the dataflow label between two entities.
- Showing invalid dataflows such as a dataflow between two data stores without a process or dataflow from an eternal entity (user) to the data store.
- DFD at higher level is not matching with the lower-level DFD or FDD or vice versa.

3.4   Data Dictionary

A data dictionary is a repository of elements in a system in an organized form. It contains systematic information regarding external entities, data stores, dataflows, and processes. Often the data dictionary is compiled by Systems Analyst manually or by Computer-Aided Systems Engineering (CASE) tool automatically in parallel to the systems development.

3.4.1   Uses of Data Dictionary

Data dictionary does not only document and manage the details regarding the systems development but also serves a mean of cross verification and communication during the systems development process. Simultaneously, it helps in the development process by providing every detail of the systems component to the Systems Analyst on need. Here are some uses of data dictionary:

Table 3.2 Components of data dictionary

Component	Subcomponents	Examples
Data elements	Data names	Employee name, employee code, file number, date of birth, etc.
	Data descriptions	Description of the data names defined is explained here. For example, a product code such as LED39_MAR_17 can be described as LED Television of 39 inches manufactured in March 2017
	Aliases	Synonyms of data names are listed here. For example, date of birth is also identified as birth date
	Length	The maximum length of the permissible values for a data name is referred here. For example, the employee number must be of five digits including its branch code
	Permissible values or ranges	The valid range or values are referred here. For example, the number of semesters for a student in a year must be 2. The value in month (in a date) field must be between 1 and 12
Data structure	Sequential relationship	First name, middle name, and surname of the employee's name follow a sequential structure
	Selection relationship	If the employee opts for a quarter (housing) facility, he is not given the housing allowance. This is an example of the selection relationship. This is also called "either–or" relationship
	Iteration relationship	Student's marks for every subject, normally six or more subjects, occur in repetitive fashion. A subject mark has internal marks, external marks, and quizzes/seminar marks. This structure is repeated for all six subjects. This is an example of iterative relationship
	Optional relationship	The field of loan installment amount in an employee pay slip is optional, as every employee might not have taken a loan from the company

- Manages details
- Documents information about systems components
- Facilitates analysis and other systems development activities
- Serves as a platform for testing and cross verification by locating errors and omissions
- Communicates with the developers and users

3.4.2   Components of Data Dictionary

Data dictionary typically encompasses data elements and data structures. Data element includes data names, data descriptions, aliases, length, and permissible values or ranges. Data structure in data dictionary may have various forms such as sequential relationship, selection relationship, iteration relationship, and optional relationship. Table 3.2 provides example(s) of each category.

3.5 Functional Approach and Object-Oriented Approach

As discussed earlier in this chapter, if a system is big and complex, it needs to be divided into modules for ease of development and control. If a system is divided into modules according to its main functionalities, then it is called function (procedure)-oriented division. If the system is divided into modules according to main entities (such as classes and objects), then the approach is called an object-oriented division.

Consider a case of the library management system (LMS) which is divided into modules according to main functionalities such as Log in and Registration functionality, Issue and return (transaction) functionalities, and Report providing functionalities. Such module division is provided in the form of a functional hierarchy chart or a function decomposition diagram (FDD). Considering the FDD as a baseline, systems detail dataflow (DFDs) and design diagrams are developed.

In case of object-oriented development of system, the library management system (LMS) is divided into modules (classes) according to main entities such as Users, Material, and supporting Infrastructure. The classes are then encapsulated with necessary methods. For example, the Material class is encapsulated with method such as Issue( ) and Return( ). To represent object-oriented paradigm, Unified Modeling Language (UML) diagrams are used. Later in this book, these concepts are discussed.

3.6 Practice Questions

3.6.1 What Is Structured Approach for Systems Development?

Many real-life systems are complex and big. These two characteristics of a system make the development of the system difficult. It would be easy if the system is partitioned into some modules and then taken into consideration for development. Each component of a system is developed with ease and control because of its reduced size and complexity. Once all the modules are developed, they are combined for an integrated solution. Such divide and conquer technique is very organized and structured, hence called structured development technique. Another advantage of the structured development approach is the ability to work in parallel. Once system is divided into components, they can be considered for parallel development.

The structured development approach includes structured analysis and structured design. Structured analysis focuses on identifying facts of the system and limitations of the system in order to find out new systems requirements. It focuses on "what" the new system should provide to overcome limitations of the existing system. Structured design focuses on "how" these limitations are met, and identified limitations of the system can be implemented.

Structured development depends on graphic description. To study the existing systems working and to demonstrate new systems model and design, diagrams like function hierarchical diagram, data flow diagrams, and Unified Modeling Language (UML)-based diagrams are used. Other important components include data dictionary, rules and procedure, and process description.

3.6.2 Define Function Hierarchy Charts with Its General Structure

A function hierarchy chart shows decomposition of system into modules using a treelike structure. It is a kind of top-down design that considers system as its root level and breaks down the system into modules. The modules are further divided into sub-modules. It generally specifies high-level design of the system; hence, it is also called high-level design. Since it decomposes the system into possible modules, it is also known as function decomposition diagram (FDD). Such diagram can show size and complexity of the system, number of modules in it, and coupling (relationship) between the modules in hierarchical fashion. The system should be decomposed in such a way that most of its modules have minimal dependency on each other. See Fig. 3.1 for general structure of a function decomposition diagram (FDD).

3.6.3 Give an Example of Function Decomposition Diagram/ Function Hierarchy Chart for Typical Bank Transaction System Managing Login, Balance Inquiry, Withdraw, and Deposit Operation

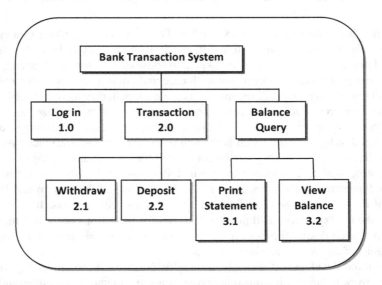

Fig. 3.5 Function decomposition diagram for typical bank transaction system

3.6.4 What Is the Use of Function Hierarchy Chart/ Decomposition Diagram (FDD)?

The function decomposition diagram (FDD) serves as follows:

- It generally specifies high-level design of the system.
- Such diagram can show size and complexity of the system, number of modules in it, and coupling (relationship) between the modules in hierarchical fashion.
- The function decomposition diagram (FDD) outlines the data flow diagram (DFD) design. According to FDD modules, processes of the DFD can be design.

3.6.5 What Are the Symbols for the DFD?

DFDs consist of four major components: entities, processes, data stores, and dataflows. There are two notation schemes for the same: Yourdon and Constantine (1979) and Gane and Sarson (1977) representation. These notations are illustrated in Table 3.1, and further details and symbols by these two methods are provided.

3.6.6 What Is DFD? What Is Context-Level DFD? Explain with an Example of a Context-Level DFD

To understand the existing system, understanding the dataflow in the business/system is a must. Which data are used, who uses these data, what data are entered, and what data is leaving the system must be known to understand the existing system and to design a new solution. The dataflow can be shown pictorially to understand, to demonstrate, and to communicate the working of a system. Such diagram is known as a data flow diagram (DFD). DFDs model system's detail by showing how input data is transformed into output results through a sequence of functional transformations. At initial point of systems development, the DFD is generally made to understand the existing physical system. After thorough study of the system, a logical systems model is developed on paper and analyzed covering limitations of the existing system. This is conceptual design of the new system. Based on the conceptual design, a physical design (DFD) of the proposed system is developed. The development procedure starts with the existing physical system, develops new logical system, and completes with physical systems.

DFDs consist of four major components: entities, processes, data stores, and dataflows. There are two notation schemes for the same: Yourdon and Constantine (1979) and Gane and Sarson (1977) representation. These notations are illustrated in Table 3.1.

The context-level data flow diagram shows all possible inputs and outputs with the system with external entities and resources. The lower-level DFDs must match

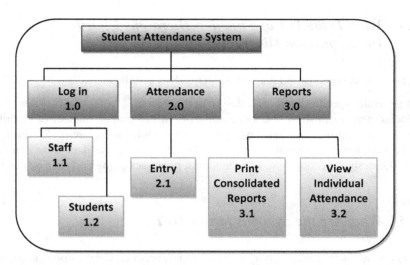

Fig. 3.6 Context-level diagram of typical student attendance system

with the context-level DFD. The context-level diagram of typical student attendance system is as follows (Fig. 3.6).

3.6.7 What Are the Advantages of DFD?

DFDs and FDDs are helpful in many ways. Some of the uses are listed below:

- To understand (analyze) working of existing system
- To demonstrate design of new system
- To communicate the design to the users and developers
- To discuss and review the design of the proposed system
- To isolate areas for better focusing, as DFDs and FDDs follow a hierarchical representation
- To cross verify the outputs at the end to satisfy the users' demand while testing
- To document the design for future use

3.6.8 What Are the Common Mistakes While Developing a Data Flow Diagram?

The common mistakes while developing a data flow diagram are summarized as follows:

- Forgetting label on any entity, especially forgetting the dataflow between two entities.
- Showing invalid dataflows such as a dataflow between two data stores without a process or dataflow from an eternal entity (user) to the data store.
- DFD at higher level is not matching with the lower-level DFD or FDD or vice versa.
- The DFDs should not contain time or control information; for this purpose flow-charts are useful.

These mistakes are illustrated in Table 3.3.

3.6.9   Differentiate Physical and Logical DFD

Major differences between logical and physical DFDs are as follows.

Logical DFDs	Physical DFDs
Logical DFD is an implantation-independent view of the current system	Physical DFD is the implementation-dependent view of the current system
Logical DFD focuses on the flow of data between processes and focuses on conceptual working of the system instead of giving importance to the physical entities related to the system	It contains physical information about the system such as people, tasks, location information, names of documents, departments, equipment, devices, and related procedures
Logical DFD is more abstract in nature (in comparison with the physical DFDs)	Physical DFDs are comparatively more specific

3.6.10   Define Data Dictionary. What Are the Main Components of the Data Dictionary?

A data dictionary is a repository of elements of a system in an organized form. It contains systematic information regarding external entities, data stores, dataflows, and processes. Often the data dictionary is compiled by Systems Analyst manually or through software.

The main components of a data dictionary are data elements and data structures. Data element includes data names, data descriptions, aliases, length, and permissible values or ranges. Data structure in data dictionary sequential relationship, selection relationship, iteration relationship, and optional relationship. Table 3.2 provides for example of each category.

Table 3.3 Mistakes while developing DFDs

Wrong practice	Correct practice

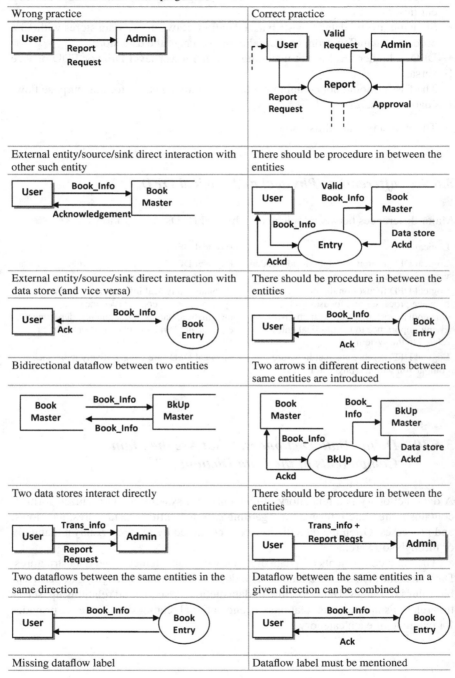

Wrong practice	Correct practice
External entity/source/sink direct interaction with other such entity	There should be procedure in between the entities
External entity/source/sink direct interaction with data store (and vice versa)	There should be procedure in between the entities
Bidirectional dataflow between two entities	Two arrows in different directions between same entities are introduced
Two data stores interact directly	There should be procedure in between the entities
Two dataflows between the same entities in the same direction	Dataflow between the same entities in a given direction can be combined
Missing dataflow label	Dataflow label must be mentioned

3.6.11 What Are the Uses of Data Dictionary?

Following are the major uses of data dictionary:

- Manages details
- Documents information about systems components
- Facilitates analysis
- Serves as a platform for testing and cross verification by locating errors and omissions
- Communicates with the developers and users

3.6.12 Examples of FDD and DFD

3.6.12.1 Library Management System (Figs. 3.7, 3.8, 3.9 and 3.10)

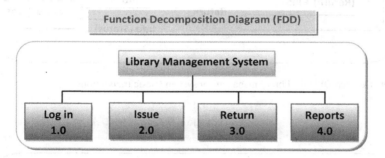

Fig. 3.7 FDD for library management system

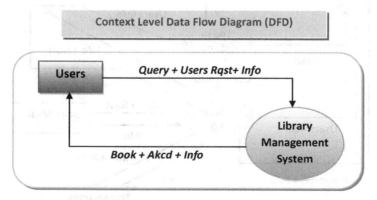

Fig. 3.8 Context-level DFD for library management system

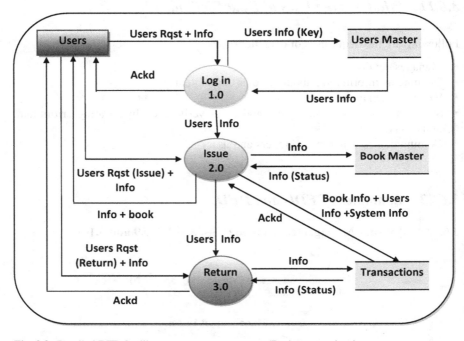

Fig. 3.9 Detailed DFD for library management system (Basic transactions)

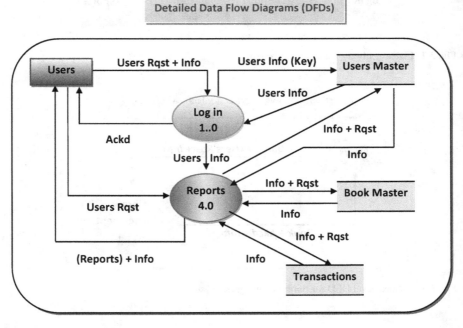

Fig. 3.10 Detailed DFD for library management system (Reports)

3.6.12.2 Outdoor Dispensary Management Systems (Figs. 3.11, 3.12, 3.13 and 3.14)

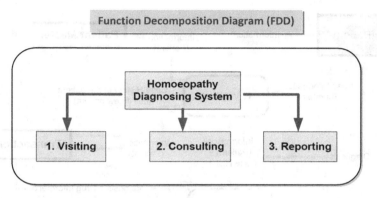

Fig. 3.11 FDD for homeopathy diagnosing system

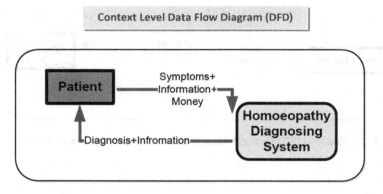

Fig. 3.12 Context-level DFD for homeopathy diagnosing system

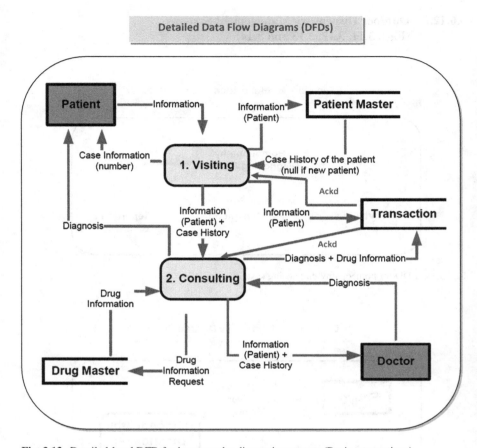

Fig. 3.13 Detailed-level DFD for homeopathy diagnosing system (Basic transactions)

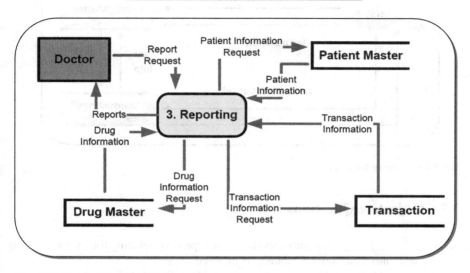

Fig. 3.14   Detailed-level DFD for homeopathy diagnosing system (Reports)

3.6.13   Given Below Is an Example of a DFD Block Regarding Online Ticket Reservation System. Identify Error(s) in the DFD Block, if Any (Fig. 3.15)

The following is the list of errors in the above DFDs:

1. Missing dataflow label from user to transaction data store.
2. There should not be any direct connection between source (external) entity (here "Users") and data store (here Transactions) without a proper process in between.
3. Similarly, the "Users" are not eligible to directly query the "Ticket Master" without a proper process.
4. Two data stores "Ticket_Master" and "Transactions" cannot interact directly.

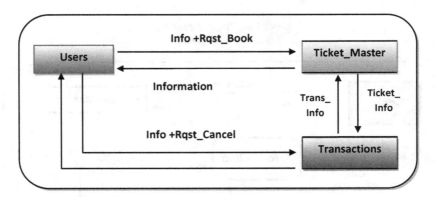

Fig. 3.15 Errors in the DFD

3.7 Objective Questions

3.7.1   In _____ systems development approach, splitting the overall task into well-defined subtasks is justified.
  (a) SDLC   (c) Structured
  (b) Prototype   (d) Agile

3.7.2   Which of the following is not a graphical tool for structured systems development?
  (a) DFD   (c) Structured interview
  (b) Context-level DFD   (d) FDD

3.7.3   The main purpose of a DFD is to specify _____ between systems components.
  (a) Relation   (c) Strength
  (b) Flow of data   (d) Flow of control

3.7.4   The _____ gives information about relationship between modules of the system and degree of cohesion of the model.
  (a) Test case diagram   (c) Entity relation diagrams
  (b) Structured chart   (d) Flow chart

3.7.5   In structured analysis and design, a big and complex system is divided into modules by considering main _____ of the system.
  (a) Objects   (c) Functions
  (b) Classes   (d) Parameters

3.7.6   In object-oriented analysis and design, a big and complex system is divided into modules by considering main _____ of the system.
  (a) Relationships   (c) Functions
  (b) Classes (or objects)   (d) Parameters

3.7.7 _____ is related with the internal strength and bond of a module and _____ is related with the relationship and dependencies between modules of the system.
- (a) Cohesion, coupling
- (b) Coupling, cohesion
- (c) Entity relation, cohesion
- (d) Any of these

3.7.8 Which of the following is the correct process to develop a new system through a structured approach?
- (a) Study the physical DFD of an existing system and develop logical DFD of the new system, and then develop physical DFD again for the new system.
- (b) Study the Logical DFD of an existing system and develop physical DFD of the new system, and then develop physical DFD again for the new system.
- (c) Study the logical DFD of an existing system, and develop the physical DFD of the new system.
- (d) Any of these

3.7.9 Which of the following is correct regarding the data flow diagram?
- (a) A dataflow may not have label.
- (b) Data can flow from a data store to another data store directly.
- (c) Data can flow from data store to external entity directly.
- (d) Data can flow from a process to a data store.

3.7.10 Full form of FDD is _____.
- (a) Functional development diagram
- (b) Function decomposition diagram
- (c) Functional data dictionary
- (d) Function database development

3.7.11 _____ DFD contains physical information such as roles/responsibilities, equipment identification, and office identification.
- (a) Conceptual
- (b) Logical
- (c) Physical
- (d) Context level

3.7.12 What is not the use of a DFD?
- (a) Communication and presentation
- (b) Understanding and analyzing
- (c) Demonstrate design
- (d) Test case generation

3.7.13 Which of the following is not a basic element of structured development of an information system?
- (a) Graphic description
- (b) Data dictionary
- (c) Data flow diagram
- (d) None of these

3.7.14 Which of the following DFD presents an implementation-independent view of the system under development?
- (a) Logical
- (b) Physical
- (c) Context level
- (d) Temporal

3.7.15 Developing a description of the system using structured analysis
follows a _____ process.
(a) Top down   (c) Hybrid
(b) Bottom up   (d) Temporal

3.7.16 _____ is the common mistake observed
while developing a DFD.
(a) Directly linking process   (c) Forgetting labels
and data store
(b) Directly linking process   (d) None of these
and external entities

3.7.17 A DFD must not contain _____.
(a) Control information   (c) Data store
(b) Data labels   (d) External entities

3.7.18 A _____ is a repository of all elements in a system
in an organized form.
(a) DFD   (c) Data dictionary
(b) FDD   (d) None of these

3.7.19 Data dictionary is used for _____.
(a) Facilitating analysis   (c) Documentation support
(b) Managing details   (d) All of these

3.7.20 Which of the following is not a component of data dictionary?
(a) Data structure   (c) Users description
(b) Data elements   (d) None of these

Answers

3.7.1	Structured	3.7.2	Structured interview
3.7.3	Flow of data	3.7.4	Structured chart
3.7.5	Functions	3.7.6	Classes (or objects)
3.7.7	Cohesion, coupling	3.7.8	Study the physical DFD of an existing system and develop logical DFD of the new system, and then develop physical DFD again for the new system.
3.7.9	Data can flow from a process to a data store	3.7.10	Function decomposition diagram
3.7.11	Physical	3.7.12	Test case generation
3.7.13	None of these	3.7.14	Logical
3.7.15	Top down	3.7.16	Forgetting labels
3.7.17	Control information	3.7.18	Data dictionary
3.7.19	All of these	3.7.20	None of these

References

Gane C, Sarson T (1977) Structured systems analysis: tools and techniques. Mcdonnell Douglas Information, St. Louis

Yourdon E, Constantine L (1979) Structured design: fundamentals of a discipline of computer program and systems design. Prentice Hall, New Jersey

References

Chapter 4
Systems Prototype Approach

Abstract This chapter describes prototype as a tool for information systems development. After introducing the application prototype development along with its characteristics, concept of prototype is discussed in detail by giving its steps in pictorial manner. The chapter also highlights other uses and advantages of the prototyping such as feasibility analysis and requirements collection besides the systems development. To develop prototype, various strategies are employed by the developers. The chapter discusses these strategies in detail. Misconception regarding prototype is also discussed in this chapter. The chapter also highlights possible applications and situations where prototype is really helpful. Tools that can be used to develop prototype through various strategies are also discussed in this chapter. At the end, chapter presents practice questions and objective questions with answers.

4.1 Application Prototype Development

Prototype is described as a preliminary working version of a system or an entity. It is an early model of system showing design and working of the system. Prototype of a system can be in any form; it may be on paper (conceptual prototype) or working model (physical prototype) of the system. Conceptual prototypes are illustrative in nature; whereas the physical prototypes are considered as either functional or simulated prototypes. Many authors consider prototype as a throwaway (disposable) models of system created as an experiment, which will be used to view and test the system, orient the users toward the use of system, and encourage sharing

Table 4.1 Characteristics
of the prototype approach

It is a quick and iterative approach for systems development
It can start with known requirements
It can be modified and reused with added requirements
It can be used as requirement elicitation as well as feasibility testing tool
Users are actively involved in the systems development process
It is comparatively less expensive to build

necessary requirements from user side. Some authors categorize prototypes as patched-up prototype, nonoperational prototype, first-of-a-series prototype, and selected feature prototype. All types of prototype are evolutionary in nature, because it is always possible to modify the prototype and test repetitively.

Prototyping is considered as a quick and iterative development of a system by building its working model. It is an alternative to the systems development approaches such as classical Systems Development Life Cycle (SDLC) approach and structured systems development (SSD – it is also known as SSADM, Structured Systems Analysis and Design Method) approach. Unlike these two approaches, the prototype offers addition of requirements and modifying the design at every iteration of the systems development process. Further, it is a quick process, where at the earliest, users can see the working of the system. Following section describes steps of prototyping. Table 4.1 enlists the main characteristics of prototype.

Because of its iterative nature, the prototype model has become very popular. Besides the prototyping, many related approaches/models are being popular. One of them is rapid application development (RAD). RAD gives little emphasis on typical analysis and design process but encourages rapid development of the working model. Another such approach is "agile" development. The agile development encourages quick development of systems procedures in small parts using extreme programming (to handle dynamic requirements) and scrum (lightweight process framework) techniques.

4.2 Steps of Prototyping

Prototyping begins with collection of the known requirements. This is the very first step of the prototyping. Both the Systems Analyst and users collect available requirements and document them formally. As stated earlier, requirements of a system determine the skeleton of the system being developed. If good requirements are identified, the system will shape according to the requirements and may result in good-quality system. However, quality is a result from the good systems design.

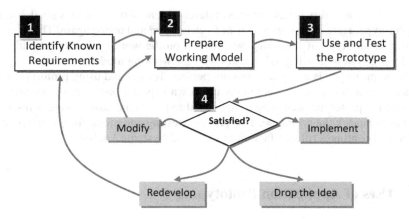

Fig. 4.1 Steps of prototyping

Users and Systems Analyst both together identify objective of the system, basic input/output, selected functionalities, data required, and other requirements. Figure 4.1 illustrates different steps of prototype approach.

Second step of prototyping is to build a working model using the collected requirements. If a system is being developed for noncomputer professional, then it may be possible that only the interface is designed. Sometimes only main functionalities of the system are simulated for demonstration. Often, system without any interface is first developed, particularly when users are technically literate fellows. There are tools available to develop prototype of a system. Programming languages (such as fourth-generation programming languages), reporting tools, Computer-Aided Software Engineering (CASE) tools, etc. are a few popular tools for prototyping.

While developing the working model of the system, users are involved with the development process; however, the responsibility of the development is generally on the Systems Analyst or the developer committee.

During the third step of the prototyping, users take lead role. It is the responsibility of users to use and evaluate prototype under guidance of the Systems Analyst. There are a number of users; each evaluates prototype according to individual perspectives and requirements.

Final stage of the prototype development is to review the prototype. If the working model (prototype developed) is perfect and satisfies every user, it can be *directly implemented*. However, no such perfect prototype is made generally. The main reason is that prototype has started with known and available requirements, not all requirements. Further, many prototypes are created to extract more requirements by giving demonstration of how system would work.

Other possibility is to *drop the idea of development of the system* and throw the prototype. By developing prototype, Systems Analyst and users have checked various feasibility issues. If the outcome is not positive, and if it seems that the resulting system would not be feasible anyhow, the idea of developing system is dropped.

The third possibility is that the idea of development of the system is good, but not the prototype. Here *new prototype is to be developed* and tested again. This may be a result of any type of feasibility verification on the working model. The idea of developing system is still good, but not with the working model approach.

Often, prototype is acceptable but not perfect. Testing and using prototype open up new requirements and reveal many unknown expectations from the system. To improve the prototype according to the added requirements and making it feasible, one has to *modify the prototype*. This process (testing and modifying) is iterative in nature and continues till satisfaction of users and Systems Analyst.

4.3   Uses of Application Prototyping

Since prototype demonstrates how the intended system would work and provide live demonstration of the system before its actual delivery, it is considered as a litmus test for the system. Whether system would be accepted by users, where it is economically, operationally and technically feasible, etc. can be tested with the help of prototype. It can be considered as requirement elicitation tool. By showing working of the system, users are encouraged to provide more and more requirements. Many times, developers may not have enough domain knowledge; at that time including users in development process ensures right domain knowledge in the system. Further, users have confidence on the system as well as systems development process. Here are the major possible uses of the prototype:

- As a systems development approach
- As a feasibility testing tool
- As a requirement elicitation tool

4.4   Strategies for Development of Prototype

A prototype is a live working model of the system. It is not supposed to be complete system accommodating all requirements. Rather, prototype begins with available and known requirements of the system in order to collect more requirements from its users and test various feasibilities of the system. Many times it is necessary to provide an atmosphere and live demonstration of the system, even without developing the full-fledged system. In such cases, partial working system will serve the purpose. Such partial development may include development of *front end interface* (such as only screens), development of primary functions (without input and output interface, backup procedures, etc.), and development of only processing functions such as input, process, and output. Figure 4.2 illustrates the major strategies of prototype.

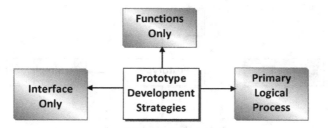

Fig. 4.2 Major strategies of prototype

For users, who do not have previous experience of using such system, development of front end interfaces (such as only screens) would be much helpful. By using such screens, users will feel at ease and starts accepting the system, even before its development. Using screens and other interfaces builds a kind of confidence among users and simulates the use of system. Users may provide additional requirements by using such screens. This strategy works best for end users who have less experience of computerized system.

The users, who are computer literate and interested in main procedures only, the strategy of developing *main primary functions*, would be appropriate. They are less interested in interface of the system. For them input/output screens and other interface-related concepts can be designed later. Further, backup utility, database preparation, etc. can also be omitted. Instead, full focus is given to selected and basic functions of the system.

There are some users, who are interested in experimenting the *complete logical flow* of the core system. For such users, input interfaces, main functions, and outputs of the system are developed as a prototype for further requirement elicitations and testing.

4.5   Misconception for Prototype

Prototype, being an iterative development process, always facilitates an opportunity to modify it frequently. This leads to the impression that the prototype is *casual and very trivial*. The prototype is neither casual nor trivial, but it is a very serious effort toward version-wise systems development with scope of improvement at each iteration.

Another myth about prototype is that the prototype is applicable for very *small and simple applications only*. This is not true at all; prototype is used when there is a high risk involved in the systems development process. Actually the prototyping should be used when the system is highly important and high degree of risk is involved with the system. The risk may be due to big volume of data and system, complexity of the system, and high cost involved in development of the system. If people are going for trail of their marriage suit (or dress), a system is far more important than that! Figure 4.3 illustrates such misconceptions.

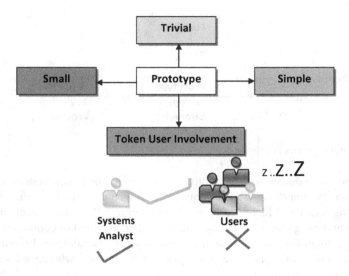

Fig. 4.3 Misconceptions about the prototype approach

Often, prototype becomes sole responsibility of the Systems Analyst (or developer). *Users are not fully involved* in using the working model. It is the responsibility of the users to evaluate the prototype and provide quality requirements and suggestions, hence involving themselves in overall development process.

4.6   Candidate Applications for the Prototype Approach

There are some applications which are novel in terms of technology and procedures. Many times users do not know how exactly the system works, as they might not have seen such system in practice. Such novel system with less known procedures and technology is the best candidate of the prototype approach. It is better to start with minimum and known requirements and to develop a working model. Users are involved at every stage of the development, especially at the evaluation phase, having their eye on the development procedure. By this way risk of using new technologies and innovative designed can be minimized. This approach can be used to monitor and control cost of the system also.

Whenever the idea is new, to test the feasibility of the idea, prototype of the system is developed and evaluated to certify various feasibilities of the system. Later, based on the feasibility evaluation done on the prototype model of the system, full-fledged system may be developed with either continuing the prototype approach or by adopting new approach such as structured approach.

In a similar manner, when full set of requirements is not formally known to the developers, the developers would like to provide a demonstration of working system in order to elicit more requirements by encouraging users.

To summarize, the following types of applications can be considered as candidate applications for the prototype development approach:

- System incorporating novel technologies and procedures, which requires user's approval.
- High-cost and high-risk type of systems.
- Requirements of the systems to be developed are not known.
- Systems that required to be checked for their feasibilities.

4.7   Tools for Prototyping

Prototyping can be done with many tools. Quick and friendly tools are considered as the best tools to develop prototype. Besides general-purpose analysis and design tools such as personal computer, programming languages, dictionary, and charting tools, tools like screen generator, report generator, ready-made and reusable code, and query languages are much useful for prototyping. Diagramming software (for data flow diagrams and UML diagrams) and dedicated Computer-Aided Software Engineering (CASE) tools are also helpful.

4.8   Practice Questions

4.8.1   Define Prototype (Also List Characteristics of Prototype)

Prototype is described as a live and preliminary version of a system showing working of the system to its users. The characteristics of the prototype are as follows:

- It can be conceptual (on paper/logical model) or working model (physical prototype) of the system.
- Prototype is developed with known requirements.
- Prototype is developed in quick manner.
- All the prototypes are iterative in nature, as newly found requirements need to be accommodated later.
- Prototype enables users' involvement in the development process.
- Prototype is used as requirements collection tool also.
- Prototype is used to test feasibility of the system under consideration. Throwaway (disposable) prototype is created to test feasibility.
- Prototype can be used as a stand-alone approach to develop an information system, and it also can be used in conjunction with other development approaches such as Systems Development Life Cycle (SDLC) approach and structured systems development (SSADM) approach.

4.8.2 Discuss Uses of Application Prototype in Brief

The prototype is meant for demonstration of working system, to test the system against users' requirements and expectations and to collect additional requirements from the system. Further, it is also used to test systems feasibility. Here is the summary of usage of prototype:

- As a systems development approach: Like Systems Development Life Cycle (SDLC) approach and structured systems development (SSADM) approach, prototype is also used to develop system. However, prototype model supports systems development process in quick and iterative manner with considerable involvement of its users.
- As a feasibility testing tool: Prototype is an actual working model in the domain; hence it provides opportunities to test its cost–benefits, ease of use, and other technical aspects involved during the development and use of the system, that is, with a valid prototype, economical, operational, and technical feasibilities can be tested.
- As a requirement elicitation tool: Live working model of the system encourages users to utilize the system and help in digging out additional as well as hidden requirements from the users' side.

4.8.3 Which Applications Are Suitable for Prototype Approach?

Here is the list of situations where prototype can be helpful:

- In novel applications, where requirements need approval: For systems which are novel in terms of techniques and procedures, at every cycle, users are there to certify working of the system. Users provide necessary requirements and suggestions and also guarantee the acceptance of the system for operation to some extent.
- High cost and risk are involved: For highly ambitious systems where high cost and risk factors are associated, prototype will be helpful. Each requirement and facility added into the system is tested and accepted by the users after checking its feasibility. This leads to easy management of cost and risks associated with the system.
- Systems for which feasibility is not sure: Prototype of the system is used to test feasibility and ensures whether the systems development is worth or not. It tests the basic objective behind the development of the system and also tests the feasibility of the system from economical, technical, and operational angle.
- To collect additional or missing requirements: In case users are not aware about the system, live model of the system may help user to build confidence about the system and encourages to provide more requirements, once they understand the working of the system.

4.8.4 Give Steps of Prototype Approach for Systems Development

The steps of the prototyping are as follows:

1. Prototyping begins with collection of known requirements. Systems Analyst and users collect available requirements and document them formally. It generally includes the objective of the system, basic input/output, selected functionalities, data required, and other requirements.
2. Build a working model using the collected requirements. The working model may be only interface, only main line functions, or selected functionalities. There are tools available to develop prototype of a system. For example, 4GL, reporting tools, Computer-Aided Software Engineering (CASE) tools, etc. can be used here.
3. Prototype is tested by its intended users. Various users evaluate the prototype under the guidance of the Systems Analyst.
4. Users may suggest some improvement and additional requirements at this stage. The following actions are possible here:

   - Accept the prototype as it is: If the prototype is perfect (which is not always), it can be accepted for final implementation.
   - Drop the idea of systems development: The prototype proves the infeasibility of the system; hence the idea of developing the system can be dropped.
   - Redevelopment of the prototype: The technique and methodology used for the prototype may not be feasible; however, it highlights the alternative mechanism with which the system can be developed. In this case prototype is redeveloped.
   - Modify the prototype: Generally, the prototype is acceptable, but not perfect. It also might have open up new ideas and requirements regarding the system. In this situation, the prototype is modified and tested again. As stated, this process (testing and modifying) is iterative in nature and continue till satisfaction of users and Systems Analyst.

   Refer Fig. 4.1 for the steps of prototype approach.

4.8.5 What Are the Strategies to Develop a Prototype? Discuss Each in Brief

A prototype is a live working model of the system. It is not supposed to be complete system accommodating all requirements. Rather, prototype begins with available and known requirements of the system in order to collect more requirements from its users and test various feasibilities of the system. Many times it is necessary to provide an atmosphere and live demonstration of the system, even without developing the full-fledged system. In such cases, partial working system will serve the purpose. Such partial development may consider the following strategies:

- Development of front end interface (such as only screens)
- Development of primary functions (without input and output interface, backup procedures, etc.)
- Development of only processing functions such as input, process, and output

    Refer Fig. 4.2 illustrating the major strategies of prototype.

4.8.6   What Are the Misconceptions About Prototype Approach for Systems Development?

The following are the major misconceptions about the prototype:

- Prototyping is casual activity: Prototype facilitates development of a system in quick and iterative manner. At the end of each cycle, it provides an opportunity to modify it. Such quick and iterative development approach gives the impression that the prototype is casual and very trivial. Instead, it is a serious effort toward systems development with scope of improvement at every iteration.
- Prototype is for small and simple applications: Prototype is used for the systems which are novel and involve high risk and with many hidden requirements. Prototype may start with known and obvious requirements, but later, many requirements will be opened up by users while reviewing the prototype. The resulting system may be highly complicated real-life system.
- User involvement is not necessary: It is the responsibility of users to review and evaluate the prototype developed under guidance of the Systems Analyst. Users must not be involved just for the sake of involvement. Rather, users should experiment the prototype thoroughly and come up with necessary suggestions, additional requirements, and decision about further action.

    See Fig. 4.3 presentation illustration of such misconceptions.

4.8.7   List Tools for Prototyping

Prototyping can be done with many tools. Tools which are helpful for analysis, design, coding, testing, and evaluation can also be used here for prototype in one or another way. However, tools which are quick and friendly are generally the best tools to develop prototype. Here is the list of some tools that can be used for prototyping:

- Personal computer
- Programming languages

- Graphic libraries and packages
- Dictionary and charting tools
- UML and DFD diagramming tools
- CASE tools
- Screen generator
- Report generator
- Query languages
- Simulation tools

4.9   Objective Questions

4.9.1   Which of the following systems development approach is adopted if information requirements are not well defined?
   (a)   SDLC   (c)   Structured approach
   (b)   Prototype   (d)   Agile

4.9.2   _____ is an iterative tool for project development which produces a live working model of the system.
   (a)   Function   (c)   Module
   (b)   Prototype   (d)   Class

4.9.3   All prototypes must be _____ in nature.
   (a)   Evolutionary   (c)   Physical
   (b)   Conceptual   (d)   None of these

4.9.4   _____ is also used as requirement finding and feasibility testing tool.
   (a)   Prototype   (c)   System
   (b)   Reports   (d)   Procedure

4.9.5   A prototype can be _____.
   (a)   Complete system with partial requirements   (c)   Full-fledged system
   (b)   Working model   (d)   All of these

4.9.6   Prototype should not be used in _____.
   (a)   Requirement not known   (c)   Novel technology
   (b)   Small and typical project with well-defined requirements   (d)   High risk

4.9.7   It is the responsibility of _____ to evaluate the prototype and suggest additional requirements, if any.
   (a)   End users   (c)   Programmers
   (b)   Analysts   (d)   Managers

4.9.8   It is the responsibility of _____ to build prototype with suitable tool.
   (a)   End users   (c)   Programmers
   (b)   Systems Analyst   (d)   Managers

4.9.9   Which of the following is not a characteristic
        of prototype?
        (a) It is quick   (c) It is reusable
        (b) It is relatively   (d) None of these
             less expensive
4.9.10 _____ is an iterative tool for project development
        which produces a live working model of the system.
        (a) Function   (c) Module
        (b) Prototype   (d) Class
4.9.11 Prototype begins with_____.
        (a) Collection of known   (c) Evaluation of prototype
             requirements
        (b) Rigorous and formal   (d) None of these
             requirement elicitation
4.9.12 After evaluation of a prototype, which of the following
        actions are possible?
        (a) Accepting prototype   (c) Throw away
             and implementing it   the prototype build
        (b) Suggesting modification   (d) All of these
             and improving
             the prototype
4.9.13 Which of the following can be used as a prototype tool?
        (a) 4GL   (c) Screen generator
        (b) Report generator   (d) All of these
4.9.14 To develop a prototype sometimes _____.
        (a) Only screens and interface   (c) Backup and security
             of the system are developed   procedures are designed
        (b) Only validations on users   (d) None of these
             input are designed
4.9.15 Prototype is _____.
        (a) Quick   (c) Reusable
        (b) Iterative   (d) All of these

Answers

4.9.1	Prototype	4.9.2	Prototype
4.9.3	Evolutionary	4.9.4	Prototype
4.9.5	All of these	4.9.6	Small and typical project with well-defined requirements
4.9.7	End users	4.9.8	Systems Analyst
4.9.9	None of these	4.9.10	Prototype
4.9.11	Collection of known requirements	4.9.12	All of these
4.9.13	All of these	4.9.14	Only screens and interface of the system are developed
4.9.15	All of these		

Chapter 5
Computer-Assisted Tools for Software Development

Abstract The chapter "Computer-Assisted Tools for Software Development" introduces concept of tools and discusses advantages of using tools, such as ease of doing the intended tasks; increase in productivity, efficiency, and quality; etc. Automation of such tools gives many advantages above these. The chapter discusses these advantages of automated tools. Further, the chapter also classifies tools in various categories such as front end, back end, and integrated tools with sufficient details. The chapter introduces Computer-Aided Software Engineering (CASE) tool with its components by giving its architecture. The chapter concludes by giving advantages and disadvantages of a CASE tool. At the end of the chapter, practice questions as well as objective questions with answers are provided.

5.1 Tools and Advantages Related to the Tools

Tool is any device or mechanism which makes some tasks possible and more effective and efficient. Here are a few examples, considering there is no language available to communicate, not even a sign language! There is no proper way to communicate without a language, without use of signs, or without facial expressions. It is clear that without such support of language, any type of communication is not possible. Language is the tool which makes the task of communication possible. Similarly, if there is no saw available, how wood can be cut into a fine sheet. You can always cut the wood, but it would not be as fine as required. Obviously, we cannot use hammer to cut the wood! Language, wheel, paper, needle, and knife are a few more examples of tool. Here are some benefits of tools:

- Tools make some tasks possible, e.g., saw to cut wood.
- Tools increase efficiency of the tasks – the task can be done in quick and fine manner saving time and effort.
- Tools help in improving the productivity.
- Tools are more effective and help in increasing quality of solution.

5.2   Computer-Assisted Tools

Computerized tools increase efficacy of a tool. Using automation in tools decreases total time period to complete the tasks by increasing the speed in delivery of the solution. Further, physical effort would be minimized with the help of automated tool. Consider the abovementioned case of saw to cut wood. If automatic saw is used, it cuts many such pieces of wood in a very short duration. Since computer is controlling the tools mechanism, it will remember the data related to the tools operations, just like a photocopy machine that stores count of total number of copies while being used. Computerized tools are initially costly; but such tools would prove cheaper at the end as it saves time and effort. Figure 5.1 demonstrates tool and computerized tool characteristics.

The benefits of computerized tools are given below:

- Computerized tools save time because of automation.
- Computerized tools save effort.
- Computerized tools guarantee uniform and consistent procedures.
- Stores systems data for future use.

5.3   Categories of Software Development Tools

For systems analysis and design there are plenty of tools available that help in the development procedure and increases efficiency and effectiveness of the systems development. Systems development activities can be divided into main categories such as *front end activities* and *back end activities*. Some practitioners call them upper-level and lower-level activities, respectively. Initial phases of development

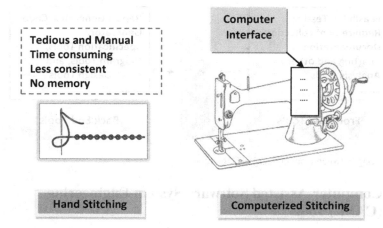

Fig. 5.1 Characteristics of tool and computerized tool

involve front end activities such as identifying preliminary information about the system, verifying various feasibilities related to the system, acquiring requirements for the system, and documenting the valid requirements in a proper form. To support these activities, tools such as fact finding methods, dictionary tools, and charting tools are available. Front end activities, especially requirement determination, play a critical role in conceiving skeleton of the system. If a system is properly analyzed and good-quality requirements are collected, then it finally lead to a high-quality system. This is the reason why the front end activities are comparatively challenging. Further, when system is implemented and post implementation review and feedback regarding the system is to be taken, front end activities/techniques will be helpful again.

On the other hand, back end activities such as designing the systems components, preparing specification for coding, testing programs, etc. are comparatively simple and have to follow the guidelines designed in analysis phase. For back end activities, tools like charting tools, database management systems, programming languages, report and query generators, testing tools, prototyping tools, etc. are used.

In spite of availability of lot of front end and back end tools, there is a requirement of a tool which can help at both the levels – at front end and at back end. The main objective of using a common tool at front and back end is not only to provide uniform interface between the phases of systems development but to reduce the gap between the front end and back end activities. Computer-Aided Software Engineering (CASE) tool is such an integrate tool. Figure 5.2 demonstrates the situation.

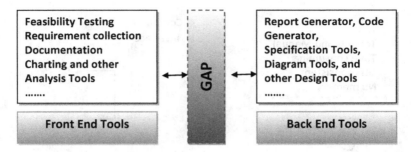

Fig. 5.2 Gap between front end and back end tools

5.4   Computer-Assisted Software/System Engineering (CASE) Tools

As stated above, the computer-supported software (or system) engineering tools are the integrated tools that support front end as well as back end activities related to the systems development. The CASE tools are inspired from computer-aided design (CAD) tools. CASE tools support systems development activities such as analysis, design, and other activities related to project management. That is, the scope of a CASE tool is throughout the systems development process. Typically a CASE tool is built around a centralized data dictionary. Surrounding the data dictionary, various supporting functionalities are available. To name a few, functionalities such as creation of systems screens, creation of database/file structure, creation of specification and charts, creation of forms for data entry and transactions, generation of reports, generation of documentation, etc. are supported through the centralized data dictionary. Figure 5.3 demonstrates these typical components of a CASE tool.

Various tools and activities supported by an integrated CASE tool are summarized in Table 5.1.

5.5   Advantages of CASE Tools

CASE tool being a computerized tool offers advantages of automation. Apart from the advantages of the automation, the CASE tool offers an integrated and holistic support to the systems development activities in uniform manner. Front end tools support activities during analysis to design phase, and back end tools support activities from design construction to implementation of a system. CASE tools try to fill the gap and extend support from analysis to implementation of the system. CASE tools help in improving quality and efficiency of the systems development process and accelerate efficient development as well as maintenance of the system. Table 5.2 summarizes the advantages of the CASE tools.

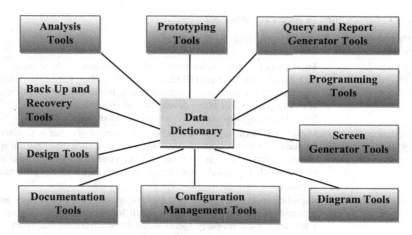

Fig. 5.3 Typical components of a CASE tool

5.6 Weaknesses of CASE Tools

CASE tools are specialized tools and many of them are not free. Further, it requires initial efforts and time for setting it up before its use. Such tools are not much useful when systems development does not follow structured approach. Rather CASE tools are much suitable for the system following the structured approaches and utilize diagrams.

All the components of a CASE tool depend on its centralized data dictionary; if the centralized data dictionary is lost, further development activities may get affected. If such data dictionary is kept on public environment such as Web without proper security measures, the data may also be in risk.

Each CASE tool has its own capacity and strategy, according to which it supports various phases of systems development in different capacities. Some CASE tools focus on analysis, some on design, and some on coding and specification. Further, every CASE tool has its own way to handle diagrams supporting systems development.

Standards for an ideal CASE tool are also needed to be considered. There should be a set of standards which can be considered as a measure of quality to check the performance of the CASE tool.

It is to be noted that the system analysis is art as well as science; hence complete automation of the development procedure is not possible and no one should expect it! Table 5.3 summarizes the weaknesses of CASE tools.

Table 5.1 Support from an integrated CASE tool

Tool/activities supported	Description
Diagram tools	These tools support development of diagrams related to the systems such as data flow diagram (DFD), Uniform Modeling Language (UML) diagrams, flow charts, and structured charts. It also supports verification of the diagrams while being developed and also checks that the lower-level diagrams are in line with upper-level diagrams or not
Programming tools	Many CASE tools support automatic development of codes in various capacities. One of the prerequisites for automatic code development is the availability of design in the form of diagrams, class files (in case of object-oriented approach), and functions signature (in case of structured approach)
Reporting tools	Reporting tools collect data from various sources such as databases and files and present the information in a well-formatted compiled report. There are some third-party agents available which collect data from homogeneous data sources and generate automatic reports. Jasper report (open-source java reporting software) and crystal report (commercial reporting software) are examples of such reporting tools
Screen/form generator tools	These tools help in generating default screens (forms) containing the fields specified in the database (data store) as mentioned in the data dictionary of the project. Later some of them may be deleted, reformatted, or rearranged
Documentation tools	Documentation of a project starts immediately with the preliminary investigation of the project and continues even after the end of the project. Data dictionary, input/output interfaces, test cases, and manuals should be well prepared and kept available even after completion of the project. Most of the CASE tools support efficient documentation support
Analysis tools	These tools support activities such as requirements acquisition, requirements specification and automatic cross verification of inconsistency in the formally specified requirements
Design tools	These tools support the development of the framework (skeleton) of the software. Various design principles such as cohesion, coupling, number of modules, etc. are considered by these tools while developing the design
Configuration tools	These tools support version and configuration management of the software system being developed
Prototyping tools	Such tools help in creating working software or a model of the system, which can be further fine-tuned. The model can also be used to test the feasibility of the system or to collect additional requirements of the system
Web-related tools	These tools support the development of Web-related facilities in a project. For example, tools for blogging, mailing, and sharing can be considered in this category. It may include specific tools for modern cloud-based system such as ready-made Web services and middleware services
Quality assurance tools	By considering various quality parameters and standard measures, such tools assure quality of the software

(continued)

Table 5.1 (continued)

Tool/activities supported	Description
Maintenance tools	Error reporting, error ticket generations, managing manuals and documentation, and other activities are taken care by maintenance tools. Many tools in this category also help in preparing for post implementation reviews through fact finding methods such as questionnaires
Backup and recovery tool	CASE tools also support backup and recovery facility in either online or offline manner

Table 5.2 Advantages of CASE tools

Uniform interface throughout the development activities
Advantages related to centralized data dictionary
Uniform data are available at common central place, which can be used for documentation and knowledge management
No redundancy of data
Change is reflected to all the components immediately
Increased reusability
Supports iterative process and easy revision
Quick support of generation of screen, code, specification, etc.
Efficient data transferability
Integration of development activities
Imparting quality and efficiency in systems development process

Table 5.3 Weakness of the CASE tools

Depends on data dictionary, if it is damaged or lost, systems development activities are affected
Dependency on structured approach
Not suitable to the system where structured approach (or diagrams) is not used
CASE tools provide limited functionalities in a limited scope
Standards for CASE tool are not well defined
Complete automation of development procedures is not possible

5.7 Practice Questions

5.7.1 Define Tool (Also Provide Summary of Advantages Offered by Tool)

Tool is any device or mechanism which makes some tasks possible and more effective and efficient. Language, wheel, paper, needle, and knife are a few examples of tool. Here are some benefits of tools:

- Tools make some tasks possible, e.g., language to communicate.
- Tools increase efficiency of the tasks – the task can be done in quick and fine manner saving time and effort.
- Tools help in improving the productivity.
- Tools are more effective and quality of solution is increased.

5.7.2 What Are the Benefits of Using Computer-Assisted Tools?

Computerized tools increase efficacy of a tool. Using automation in tools decreases total time period to complete the task and increases the speed in the delivery of the solution. Further, physical effort would be minimized with the help of automated tool. It will also remember the data related to the tools operations, which can be used later on for future decision-making. Computerized tools are initially costly; but such tools would prove cheaper at the end as it saves time and effort. The benefits of computerized tools are given below:

- Save time due to automation.
- Save effort as risky and tough manual processes have been automated.
- Provide guarantee of uniform and consistent procedures.
- Store systems data for future use.

   Refer to Fig. 5.1 for example.

5.7.3 Describe Categories of Software Development Tools (Also Provide Example of Each Category)

Software development tools are divided as per the systems development activities, which are *front end activities* (upper level) and *back end activities* (lower level).
   Front end tools support front end activities such as:

- Collection of factual data
- Requirement investigation
- Specification of valid requirements into proper form
- Work flow management
- Data dictionary management

   Examples of front end tools are fact finding methods, dictionary tools, and charting tools.
   Tools under back end categories support back end activities such as:

- Modeling and system design
- Detailed design of the systems components

- Preparation of specification for coding
- Coding
- Designing of testing strategies and test cases

These activities are supported by back end tools like charting tools, database management systems, report and query generators, testing tools, prototyping tools, etc.

CASE tool is a kind of integrated tool. Its main objective is to meet gap between the front end and back end activities via uniform interface. Example of such tools is Rational Rose.[1] Various other tools are mentioned on the website Tigris.org.[2] It is a website providing support for collaborative software development. Some of its current projects are on automated source code analysis, metrics, and related tools; coding, testing, and debugging tools; software requirements management tools; software testing automation tools; etc.

5.7.4   Define CASE (Which Type of Tool Is It? What Benefits Does It Offer?)

Full form of CASE is Computer-Assisted Software (or System) Engineering. CASE is an integrated tool that supports front end as well as back end activities related to the systems development. Front end activities like collection of factual data, requirements investigation, specification of valid requirements into proper form, work flow management, and data dictionary management, etc. are managed by a CASE tool. Apart from these, the back end activities such as modeling and system design, detailed design of the systems components, preparation of specification for coding, designing of testing strategies and test cases, coding, reporting, etc. are also supported by a CASE tool.

CASE tools support majority of the activities related to project management in an integrated fashion with uniform interface and centralized data dictionary. The scope of a CASE tool is throughout the systems development process. Typically a CASE tool is built around a centralized data dictionary. Surrounding the data dictionary, various supporting functionalities are available. To name a few, functionalities such as creation of systems screens, creation of database/file structure, creation of specification and charts, creation of forms for data entry and transactions, generation of reports, generation of documentation, etc. The following are the major benefits of a CASE tool:

- Uniform interface throughout the development activities
- Advantages related to centralized data dictionary:
  - Uniform data are available at common central place, which can be used for documentation and knowledge management.

---

[1] http://www-03.ibm.com/software/products/en/enterprise
[2] http://www.tigris.org/

- No redundancy of data.
- Change is reflected to all the components immediately.
- Increased reusability.

• Supports iterative process and easy revision
• Quick support for generation of screen, code, specification, etc.
• Efficient data transferability
• Integration of development activities
• Imparting quality and efficiency in systems development process

5.7.5   Draw General Diagram of a Typical CASE Tool (Also Describe All Its Components in One-to-Two Lines Each)

The general diagram of a CASE tool is given in Fig. 5.3.

Various tools and activities supported by an integrated CASE tool are summarized as follows.

Diagram Tools These tools support development of diagrams related to the systems such as data flow diagram (DFD), Uniform Modeling Language (UML) diagrams, flow charts, and structured charts. It also supports verification of the diagrams while being developed and also checks that the lower-level diagrams are in line with upper-level diagrams.

Programming Tools Many CASE tools support automatic development of codes in various capacities from properly documented design of the system. One of the prerequisites for automatic code development is the availability of design in the form of diagrams, class files (in case of object-oriented approach), and functions signature (in case of structured approach). A CASE tool may support test case generation as per logic design of the generated code.

Reporting Tools Reporting tools collect data from various sources such as databases and files and present the information in a well-formatted compiled report. There are some third-party agents available which collect data from homogeneous data sources and generate automatic reports. Jasper report (open-source java reporting software) and crystal report (commercial reporting software) are examples of such reporting tools.

Screen/Form Generator Tools These tools help in generating default screens (forms) containing the fields specified in the database (data store) as mentioned in the data dictionary of the project. Later some of them may be deleted, reformatted, or rearranged.

Documentation Tools Documentation of a project starts immediately with the preliminary investigation of the project and continues even after the end of the project. Data dictionary, input/output interfaces, test cases, and manuals should be well prepared and kept available even after completion of the project. Most of the CASE tools support efficient documentation support.

Analysis Tools These tools support activities such as requirements acquisition, requirements specification, and automatic cross verification of inconsistency in the specified requirements.

Design Tools These tools support the development of the framework (skeleton) of the software. Various design principles such as cohesion, coupling, number of modules, etc. are considered while employing such tools.

Configuration Tools These tools support version and configuration management of the software system being developed.

Prototyping Tools Such tools help in creating working software or a model of the system, which can be used to test the feasibility of the system or to collect additional requirements of the system.

Web-Related Tools These tools support the development of Web-related facilities such as mail facility in a project.

Quality Assurance Tools By considering various quality parameters and standard measures, such tools assure quality of the software.

Maintenance Tools Error reporting, error ticket generations, managing manuals and documentation, and other activities are taken care by maintenance tools. Many tools in this category also help in preparing for post implementation reviews through fact finding methods such as questionnaires.

Backup and Recovery Tool CASE tools also support backup and recovery facility in either online or offline manner.
The abovementioned components are mentioned in Table 5.1.

5.7.6   Provide Advantages of CASE Tools

The advantages of the CASE tools are as given below:
- Uniform interface throughout the development activities
- Advantages related to centralized data dictionary:

  – Uniform data are available at common central place.
  – No redundancy of data.
  – Change is reflected to all the components immediately.
  – Increased reusability.

- Supports iterative process and easy revision
- Quick support for generation of screen, code, specification, etc.
- Efficient data transferability
- Integration of development activities

5.7.7   Provide Weakness of CASE Tools

Weaknesses of CASE tools are as given below:

- Depends on data dictionary, if it is damaged or lost, systems development activities are affected.
- Depends on structured approach only.
- Not suitable to the system where structured approach (or diagrams) is not used.
- CASE tools provide limited functionalities in a limited scope.
- Standards for CASE tool are not well defined.
- Complete automation of development procedures is not possible.

5.8   Objective Questions

5.8.1   _____ is any device, procedure, or agent that, if used properly, improves efficiency of the tasks.
- (a) Program
- (b) User
- (c) Function
- (d) Tool

5.8.2   Full form of CASE is _____.
- (a) Computer-Aided Software Engineering
- (b) Comprehensive Aimed Systems Engineering
- (c) Collective All Systems Engineering
- (d) Cost Added Systems Embedding

5.8.3   Example of front end tool is _____ kind of tool.
- (a) Analysis and fact finding
- (b) Code generator
- (c) Report generator
- (d) Screen generator

5.8.4   Example of a CASE tool is _____.
- (a) Rational Rose
- (b) Turbo Analyst
- (c) Relational Designer
- (d) All of these

5.8.5   _____ is a central (core) portion of a typical CASE tool.
- (a) Database
- (b) Knowledge base
- (c) Interface
- (d) Data dictionary (DD)

5.8.6   CASE tools typically suit _____ approach of systems development.
- (a) Linear
- (b) Nonlinear
- (c) Spiral
- (d) Structured

5.8.7   CASE tools are dependent on _____, which can be its one of the limitations.
- (a) Diagrams
- (b) Standards
- (c) Developer environment
- (d) None of these

5.8.8   CASE tool is a/an _____ type of tool useful for the
systems development process.
(a) Low level   (c) Integrated
(b) High level   (d) Front end

5.8.9   To formulate logic design and actual code, _____ tools are used.
(a) Proprietary   (c) Back end
(b) High level   (d) Front end

5. 8.10 To automate early activities in systems analysis and design
_____ tools are used.
(a) Report generator   (c) Test case generator
(b) Front end or high level   (d) Screen generator

5. 8.11 Which of the following activities is not supported by CASE?
(a) Report generation   (c) Diagrams
(b) Screen generation   (d) None of these

Answers

5.8.1	Tool	5.8.2	Computer-Aided Software Engineering
5.8.3	Analysis and fact finding	5.8.4	All of these
5.8.5	Data dictionary (DD)	5.8.6	Structured
5.8.7	Diagrams	5.8.8	Integrated
5.8.9	Back end	5.8..10	Front end or high level
5.8.11	None of these		

Chapter 6
Systems Design

Abstract The chapter "Systems Design" introduces concept of information systems design along with the desirable characteristics of systems design. It lists out major elements of design such as output, input, interactions, processes, and controls. The chapter provides brief discussion on major outcomes of the systems design phases. Further, the chapter provides a brief overview on function-oriented and object-oriented systems design. While discussing output design, the chapter highlights types of output as well as things to be considered during designing output. Similarly, objective of input design, coding methods to make input efficient, and data capture guidelines are also provided in this chapter. The chapter also provides brief introduction to the design of dialogues, processing, and control. After completing the systems design process, some outputs are expected, discussion of which is also provided in this chapter. At the end of the chapter, practice questions as well as objective questions with answers are provided.

6.1 Introduction to Information Systems Design

When analysis is completed, the possible outcomes on hand are the collection of facts and problems related to the system. During the analysis phase, the concern details about the system are collected and studied well in order to find out problems and limitations of the current system. During systems analysis, emphasis is given to the fact "what are the problems"; while during systems design, focus is on "how the

Table 6.1 Major outcomes of the systems analysis phase

Outcome	Description
Formal problem statement	Formal problem statement, domain of the problem, and broad objective of the problem
Data dictionary	It is a repository of the facts and details about the current system including users, processes, diagrams including aliases, validations, data structures, exceptions, etc.
Software requirements specifications	List of valid requirements provided by various users
Feasibility reports	Feasibility reports of suggested requirements (both valid and invalid)
Special remarks	List of problems encountered so far and limitations of the existing systems
	Special requirements and choices of users
Feedback	Feedback on the documented requirements and suggestions
Conceptual systems architecture	Broad outline/conceptual architecture of the system

problems can be solved and new requirements identified can be added into the new system." At the end of the systems analysis phase, the following are the major outcomes (Table 6.1):

- Facts and details about the current system including users, processes, diagrams, and other documentations
- List of problems encountered so far and limitations of the existing systems
- Feedback of users of the system
- List of requirements identified that must be added into the new system; may be in typical Software Requirements Specification (SRS) format well signed by the authority, developers, and concern parties
- Problem statement of a new proposed system
- Feasibility test reports of the new proposed system
- Broad outline/conceptual architecture of the system. Table 6.1 enlists these outcomes.

6.2 Desirable Characteristics of a Good Design

It is the design of the system which provides the basic skeleton to the system. Good-quality system is mainly the result of its good design, not the result of testing. It is obvious to expect that the design of a system is acceptable and of good quality. The very first requirement of a systems design is that it should perform the intended business, everything expected from routine transactions to the exceptional reports, whichever falls under the scope of the system. Further, the design must be transferable to its equivalent computer code. The design must be documented properly with the help of diagrams or specifications, so that programmers and users can understand and convert it into equivalent code. The following are the desirable characteristics that can be expected from a good design:

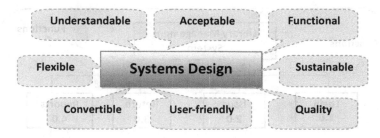

Fig. 6.1 Desirable characteristics of a good design

- The design should meet systems objectives; that is, it should be functional.
- The design should be acceptable and meet users' requirements.
- The design should be easy to understand, document, and communicate and implementable, so that coding can be done.
- The design must be user friendly and should follow quality standards.

Further, the design of a system should be sustainable, well made, and flexible enough to adopt changes (if any, in the future) in the system. Figure 6.1 illustrates the above characteristics.

6.3 Elements to Design

Majority of the real-life systems are big and/or complex. There are various factors that make systems development process challenging. Prime of them are increased scope of the system, large number of voluminous data, complex procedures, and highly ambitious expectations from the users. It is difficult to manage system as a single entity to handle and to develop. Hence, it is advisable to divide the system into parts and handle each component separately in efficient manner.

If the system is analyzed and designed into parts according to its main classes (group of similar types of objects), then the approach is called object-oriented design. However, to be a true object-oriented system, the system should behave in such a way that it supports mechanisms like encapsulation, polymorphism, and inheritance. Just by having objects in the system does not make the system object oriented!

On other hand, if the system is studied and divided into parts according to its main functions, then the approach is called the function oriented (or structured) approach. Figure 6.2 illustrates the object-oriented and function-oriented division of a typical library management system.

Once a system is divided into parts in order to design and develop them independently and later conquering an integrated solution, a broad framework showing design of system evolved. Such broad framework of systems design introducing various modules/components of the systems is known as *systems design*, broad design, or higher-level design.

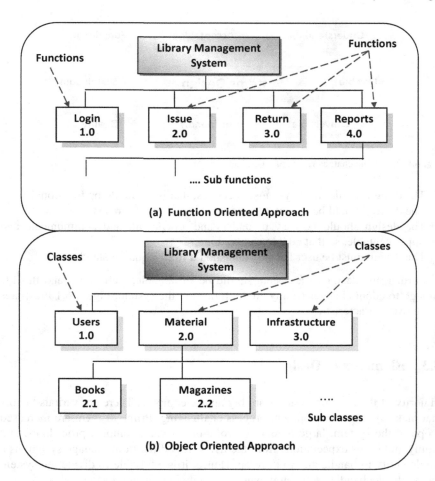

Fig. 6.2 Function-oriented and object-oriented approach

Later, while focusing on the design of individual component (class – in case of object-oriented approach or function in structured approach), detailed design can be done. The detailed design should carry sufficient details, precise, and complete so that it would be easy to translate it in its equivalent coding.

During the design phase, there are various components needed to be shaped and designed efficiently in such a way that later they can be combined in a full-fledged working system. Primary of them are input and output interface; main functionalities of the business, reports, database, and files; runtime procedures; and interaction with systems such as dialogues, validations, documentation, and manuals related to the system. Table 6.2 summarizes the major elements to be designed.

Remaining sections of this chapter describe the major components to be designed in detail.

Table 6.2 Major elements to be designed

Element	Description
Output	Output content, format, frequency, location, methodology, etc.
Input	Data collection, clearing, encoding, entry, validations, input mechanism, responsible person for input and format of input, etc.
Dialogue	Systems interaction for input, error messages, notifications and other messages to the users, etc.
Database and files	Items to be stored, format of storage, preprocessing before storing, primary and foreign keys, file organizations, concurrency control, encryption within the files and databases, normalization and backup and security, etc.
Processes	Processes supporting main business transactions, runtime processes, verification and validation processes, etc.
Documentation and manuals	Data dictionary, Software Requirements Specification, charts, specifications, user and programmer manuals, etc.
Roles	Who will take predefined responsibility, play what role, etc.

6.4 Design of Output

Output of a system is the delivery of information, triggering of event, providing acknowledgment of a task, or a mean of providing alarm about an event. The output delivered to the users must be useful, complete, and in time. Here are some *objectives of output design*:

- The output should be correct and in appropriate quantity.
- The output must be useful (required) and complete; it should convey information, which is demanded.
- The output must be distributed in time.
- Means to distribute output must be appropriate and effective.
- Correct distribution of the output must be ensured.

6.4.1 Types of Output

Output can be in the form of information, which may be in multimedia. Besides texts and numbers, information can be audio, video, and image form also. Further, the output may be in the form of action or alarm signaling an event. Multimedia information is more effective in comparison with the textual information. One should also consider the age group, abilities, and interests of target audience while using multimedia output besides the nature of the system being developed. For example, to young school children, audiovisual learning material would be much helpful in comparison with simple text-based output. In a similar manner, for specially challenged people, such as blinds, audio output is proper. For young adults, mobile short message or message on social network platform would also serve the purpose of the output.

The output can be in the form of a printed document in a variety of formats. Some possible formats are simply running plain text, tabular form, on preprinted stationery (such as letter pad and bills), special forms, images, charts, graphs, etc. in one or multiple copies. If it is a table, the information presented in it must be sorted meaningfully, and totals/subtotals of categories/items included in the table, etc. with proper heading must be there in the table. For preprinted stationery, margins, spacing, and arrangement of information should be done carefully.

Another popular form of an output is the visual output. Typically the most used tool for visual output is the monitor or projector attached with the computer. If there are other systems existing in the organization, it must follow the similar design (such as arrangement of items on screen, logos, color scheme, theme, etc.) for uniformity and better integration. All the icons (images on console) must be uniform for all output screens among all the related products/systems. For example, Microsoft Office packages Word, PowerPoint, and Excel have similar symbols and menus. Division of screen space is also an important point while designing visual output (e.g., Web page design and programming language compiler debugging screen design). Dividing the output screen into parts enables partly refreshing the screen and providing better representation of content.

Output can also be an alarm for an event. It can be a reminder for an activity or alarm to convey important information in time, when immediate action is required. Example of such output is an alarm with blinking light, indicating that the paper tray of a printer is empty and needs refill immediately to continue printing procedure.

Output of a system may not produce printed or visual output always, but it can be a form of activity such as uploading a document. However, with this activity/ action, an acknowledgment is required.

During systems input and/or processing, some intermediate outputs are also required. On visual output means/interfaces, at the time of data entry, some help text and images are also needed, which is also an important output during input phase and processing phase.

6.4.2   Things to Be Considered While Designing Output

Important things to remember while designing outputs are as follows:

- What will be the content of output? What is required?
- What is the purpose of the output?
- Who is the recipient of the output? Whether the person has access and ability to work with output devices? Do we require multiple outputs in a series on a device or parallel output to different devices?
- What is the medium of output? In which form the output is required?
- How often the output is required?
- Whether the output is used as input of other system (turnaround document). If so, will it match the next procedures for input format?

It is the good-quality output that finally impresses the users of the system and increases acceptance of the system among its users.

6.5 Design of Input

Unless the system takes some data and requests from its users, no processing is done and no output can be generated. The very important thing to consider while designing an input to a system is to determine which input is needed from the users and what would be the form of the required information. The input must be correct, efficiently provided to the system, should be free from errors, and must not be complex and error prone, as most of the users are noncomputer professionals. These objectives of the inputs are listed below.

6.5.1 Objectives of the Input

- The input must be correct; users are given prompt at appropriate place and time about which input is exactly required; if the input is wrong, system must validate it or reject it.
- The amount of input should be minimum in order to save time, effort, and errors; if input is available in any form to the system, it must not be taken from users; example is when birth date is available, users should not be asked for age. Similarly, constants and already stored information within the system must not be asked.
- The input should avoid delay.
- The process of input must be simple and user friendly.

While designing input, one must consider to encode the input to make the input mechanism efficient. For example, with every student in a college, if department and subjects of the students have to be entered, it must be codified. For example, Computer Science department code is CE and subjects are CE1E01 (Computer science, first semester, elective course number 1). Here normalization of data will also be helpful.

6.5.2 Coding Methods

As mentioned in previous section, the input coding methods are presented in the tabular manner at Table 6.3.

Table 6.3 Popular coding methods

Coding method	Description	Example
Classification code	Classifies entities into different groups	42 inch LED color television is encoded as LED42
Function code	Classifies entities according to their functionalities	A for addition, D for deletion, and M for multiplication can be used for different functions
Sequence code	Sequential numbers or letters assigned to the entities	1, 2, 3, ... or A, B, C, ... can be used to encode entities
Significant digit subset code	Each digit or group of digit has its significance	All C++ programming books purchased in 2016 can be encoded as CPP1601, where CPP is the category (first three digits), 16 is the year (middle two digits), and 01 is the serial number (last two digits)
Picture coding	Instead of number or alphabet, an image is used to label the entities	Image of star is used to indicate important entities
Color coding	Instead of number or alphabet, specific color code is used to label the entities	Colored dot is used to indicate vegetarian or nonvegetarian food items

6.5.3   Data Capture Guidelines

There are some key points that may be considered while designing an input to a system. These key considerations are given as follows:

- Which input is required? It is to be noted that the data which is already there with the system, or which can be calculated or retrieved by the system, need not be taken from the user.
- Who will provide the input?
- What is the mean of providing input to the system? Key punching at source, through online transfer, through turnaround document, through handheld terminal, etc., may be considered here, keeping a wide variety of input mechanisms in mind. That is, from which device and location input will be collected? Table 6.4 presents data capture guidelines. Captured data must be clear from noise, readable, valid, and properly encoded if needed.
- How input would be given to the system: in offline or online manner? If the input is provided in offline or batch mode, is there any cleaning and preprocessing required on it?
- Is it required to codify the big and complex input in order to simplify the input procedures? If yes, what is the coding scheme?

Once data are captured, during the input process or immediately after that, the input must be validated. Automatic correction, check digits, filed existence test, limit and range test, etc. can be considered for input validations.

Table 6.4 Data capture guidelines

Input mechanism	Characteristic
Key punching at source	Manual entry of input data using keyboard and/or mouse pointer, joystick, card, etc.
Natural language	Native English or regional language-based input
Multimedia inputs	Through devices such as scanners (images), mike (audio), touch screen, etc.
From secondary storage	Offline and previously stored data provided as input
Online transfer	Retrieval of data from remote resource
Turnaround documents	Output of another system, directly provided to the system
Intelligent terminals	A terminal which is having some processing power, generally to validate data or to preprocess data provided by users/devices
Executable programs	Online forms on Web environment

6.6 Design of Dialogues

Design of system dialogue is another important issue that needs to be taken care while designing the system. It is necessary that the system should give immediate response to the users' request. If the system is going to take some time to process the request, at least the system should say "Please wait....!" The dialogue between the system and users establishes a direct contact between the system and user; it must be friendly, easy to understand, and appealing. Many times, Systems Analyst designs very good interaction between the system and users for most obvious transactions but overlooks the less frequently occurring choices. One has to consider the less predictable demand from users too; it may be possible that an exceptional user (such as a VIP sitting on the highest post) may put an uncommon request to the system. After the input, dialogue and interaction between the systems and users are the systems interface that facilitates the use of the systems.

6.7 Design of Processing and Control

Other entities to be designed include design of processes, storage mechanism such as database and files, and design of control. Valid input from various media and locations is accepted and processed to get desired output. The process must be efficient in terms of time and memory (space) requirement and should produce the desirable output. Necessary priority management is also to be considered for scheduling of processes. If there is a dedicated hardware such as multiprocessors or parallel and/or distributed processing, it must be taken care by suitable processing mechanism. Important processes about the data entry, core business functions, error and exceptional handling, and security and backup must be designed carefully. System must ensure the proper design of authorized access of the system, acceptability of the transaction, etc. along with the design of aforementioned elements. If the system is computerized, all the designed processes must be documented in the form of program specification or formally represented in order to implement them in the form of programs.

6.8   Software Design Principles

We have seen that the design of a system is very important task and directly affects the quality of a system. Such an important phase must be supported by some principles and guidelines. This section discusses the major principles of designing the system.

Modularity and Partitioning This is very first principle that guides the systems design process. Real-life systems are big (wide) in scope and complex enough to handle. It is suggested to partition the system into modules according to major functions (function-oriented/structured-oriented approach) and according to major classes (object-oriented approach) mainly. The system is consortium of many lower-level modules which are comparatively smaller in functionality and size. It can be considered as top-down design of a system where the system is considered as a big main function, which is further divided into smaller modules. Modularity and partitioning principle helps in managing systems development processes efficiently and enables parallel development of the system. Later on, the modules developed independently and may be in parallel manner, which are afterward can be integrated for a global solution. Further, information hiding and access right permission management will be easy with the modularity and partitioned approach.

Size of the Modules It should be taken care that majority of the modules are of manageable size. Size of a module is generally referred to as number of instructions in a module. It is not advisable to have some modules very large and some are very small. In this case, large modules can be further divided into sub-modules.

Span of Control A system or module (if further divided into sub-modules) may refer to many other modules. In other words, we can say that a parent module is having control on its children modules. It is not advisable to have many children modules for a parent module. Generally, a heuristic says that a module can be divided into four to six sub-modules for a typically complex real-life application. However, it depends on the complexity and size of the parent module.

Coupling Coupling is defined as strength of relationship between the modules. The degree of coupling must be minimum to allow the modules to work (and to manage development activities) independently. If one module is failed, the system can still work with remaining modules with the limited functionality. Coupling can be reduced by controlling the parameters between modules, passing the copy of data instead of control information, and avoiding inter-module interactions. We can say that less (loose) coupling means less dependency of modules on each other. Though less coupling is desirable, one cannot make it nil as the modules are derived from a common parent system.

Table 6.5 Systems design principles

Design principles	Description
Modularity and partitioning	System is divided into lower-level modules which are smaller in scope and size to manage development processes and enable parallel development of the modules independently
Size of a module	Size of a module refers to number of instructions in the module, which must be manageable
Span of control	A system or module may refer to many other modules and has control on children modules. It is not advisable to have many children modules for a parent module
Coupling	The degree of relationship between modules must be minimum. Since the modules belong to a parent module/system, the relationship cannot be totally nil
Cohesion	Cohesion is defined as internal strength of a module or binding within a module, which must be tight. Unlike coupling, cohesion is desired to be tight and maximum
Shared use of a module	The module which offers common functionalities is often shared by many other parent modules or systems to minimize the effort required for software development, maintenance, and error handling. This feature is often considered along with coupling principle

Cohesion Cohesion is defined as internal strength of a module or binding within a module. The strength of relations within a module must be tight. The elements such as instructions, data structure, and data within the modules/functions are needed to be logically related with each other at a given instance of time. Unlike coupling, cohesion must be maximized.

Shared Modules Commonly used functionality at different places and time are generally defined once and used many times. The module which offers such common functionalities is often shared by many other parent modules or systems. Besides minimizing amount of software to be developed and maintain, it offers the advantages of minimizing the effort required for error handling too. Because of these advantages, often the shared modules are welcomed as they provide well-tested and reusable software.

Table 6.5 illustrates the design principles in brief.

Tools like structured charts, data flow diagrams, Unified Modeling Diagrams (UML), hierarchical input process output (HIPO) charts, visual table of contents and functional diagrams, Warnier/Orr diagrams, etc. can be used to document the design developed for the system.

6.9   Outputs of Design

When design phase is completed, the designer is expected to produce design documents such as structured charts, data flow diagrams, UML diagrams, layout charts, database or file record layouts, validation designs, screen and interface design, program specifications, etc. List of all activities involved in the design phase, roles and responsibilities shared by personnel, and development budget and plan also need to be prepared. Documents related to the development activities such as roles, plans, and budget are helpful in monitoring and controlling the systems design process. At the end, design must satisfy its objectives (represented in Sect. 6.2 of this chapter) and available to the programmers, testers, users, and other experts. This is the time to finalize (or reevaluate) proper hardware and software selected for the systems development.

6.10 Practice Questions

6.10.1 What Are the Deliverables of the Systems Analysis Phase?

At the end of the systems analysis phase, the following are the major outcomes and deliverables:

- Facts and details about the current system including users, processes, diagrams, and other documentations
- List of problems encountered so far and limitations of the existing systems
- Feedback of the users of the system
- List of requirements identified that must be added into the new system; may be in typical Software Requirements Specifications (SRS) format well signed by the authority, developers, and concern parties
- Problem statement of a new proposed system
- Feasibility test reports of the new proposed system
- Broad outline/conceptual architecture of the system

That is, at the end of analysis, before starting design of the proposed system, components such as formal problem statement, data dictionary, Software Requirements Specification (SRS), feasibility reports, special remarks for systems, if any, feedback and broad conceptual architecture of the proposed system should be available. Table 6.1 refers to the description of above mentioned entities.

6.10.2 What Are the Objectives (Desirable Characteristics) of the Systems Design?

The following are the desirable characteristics that can be expected from a good design:

- The design should meet systems objectives, i.e., it should be functional.
- The design should be acceptable and meet users' requirements.

- The design should be easy to understand, document, and communicate, so that coding can be done.
- The design must be user friendly and should follow quality standards.

In addition to these characteristics, the design of a system should be sustainable, well made, and flexible enough to adopt changes in the system. Refer to Fig. 6.1.

6.10.3 List Major Elements of Systems to Be Designed with Brief Description of Each

The major entity to be designed is the number of modules (either classes or functions) of the system as per the requirements finalized, which is called the broad (systems) design. Above this, the external entities, users, data stores, data flows, procedures, etc. need to be designed. Here is the list of the major items to be designed:

- Modules and their relationships
- Internal logic and procedures for the modules
- Input, output, dialogue and interaction with the users, backup and recovery, runtime error handling procedures, database and files, etc.
- Interface and screen design
- Procedure designs and specifications
- Roles and responsibilities

Refer to Table 6.2 for summary of the major elements to be designed.

6.10.4 Which Entity in a Systems Design Is Generally Designed Initially Prior to Any Other Design? Why?

Among various systems development activities, the output design should be considered first. When goal and objective of the system are well defined, then the input and procedural needs will be cleared. All the queries related to input & processing comes in picture after determining required output. To get the desired output, it is important to know the type of input needed, format of the input, and important validations. Further, how the input is processed to get the desired output is also important information that the developer would like to know.

6.10.5 Enlist a Few Objectives of the Output Design

The main objectives of output design are as given below:

- The output should be correct and in appropriate quantity.
- The output must be useful (required) and complete; it should convey information, which is demanded.

- The output must be distributed in time.
- Means to distribute output must be appropriate and effective.
- Correct distribution of the output must be ensured.

6.10.6   List Major Considerations While Designing Output of a System

Important things to remember while designing outputs are as follows:

- What will be the content of output? What is required?
- What is the purpose of the output?
- Who is the recipient of the output? Whether the person has access and ability to work with output devices? Do we require multiple outputs in a series on a device or parallel output to different devices?
- What is the medium of output? In which form the output is required?
- How often the output is required?

6.10.7   Search for Various Validations of Input Data of Your Choice (For Example, Consider the Typical Employee Information and Provide Various Validations on It)

Consider the table showing example attributes for an employee along with the list of possible validation checks on it (Table 6.6).

6.10.8   What Are the Major Types/Forms of Output from a System?

There are various forms of output by a system. The most popular output forms are as follows:

1. Information on screen such as results, information, error and help messages, etc. in multimedia format
2. Printed information such as bills, letters, and reports on various types/sizes of papers as well as preprinted stationery
3. Output to a website (information) or hardware such as alarms and signals

Table 6.6 Validations on Employee data

Field name	Description	Validation checks
Emp_no	Employee number	In suitable format such as string, integer, etc.
		If integer numbers are used, the emp_no value should not be zero, negative, and fractional
		It must not be the null value and can be primary key
Emp_name	Name of employee	Only characters and converted in capital letters
Emp_bdate	Birth date of employee	In proper date format
		Must be less than today's date
		The minimum difference between the birth date and today's date is the number of years to get the job, e.g., 24
Emp_contact	Mobile or other contact number	Must be ten digits
		With country or city code
Emp_jdate	Date of joining the organization	In proper date format
		Must be less than or equal to today's date, i.e., not in the future
Emp_bpay	Basic pay of an employee	Should not be zero or negative
		Less than or equal to the maximum basic pay in the category/slab
		Limit of minimum salary to maximum salary can be kept
Emp_gender	Gender of an employee	Value should be either male or female
		It can be character or Boolean field
Emp_status	Marital status of employee	Value should be either married or unmarried
		It can be character or Boolean field
Others	…	…

6.10.9   *Which Items Should Not Be Considered as Input to the System?*

The data which is already there with the system, or which can be calculated or retrieved by the system, need not be taken from the user. Example is, instead of asking the age of user, the system should ask about the birth date, which is more accurate and effective. Similarly, constants (e.g., value of Pi = 22/7) and facts (list of holidays) must be stored in the system.

6.10.10 What Is the Significance of Encoding the Input Data? Write Advantages of Such Encoding of Input Data with Example of Your Choice (Or Write a Note on Various Input Coding Schemes with Suitable Examples of Each Scheme)

It is better to consider encoding the input for efficient acquisition of the input from users. For example, with every student in a college, if department and subjects of the students have to be entered, it must be codified. For example, Computer Science department code is CE and subjects are CE1E01 (Computer science, first semester, elective course number 1). Such coding saves time, effort, and possibilities of errors and helps in normalization of the data. Here are some popular encoding schemes.

Classification Code This coding scheme classifies entities into different groups, example of which can be FW_D_16, for a four wheeler running on diesel and manufactured in the year 2016.

Function Code This coding scheme classifies entities according to their functionalities such as A for addition D for deletion and E for exiting from the system.

Sequence Code Sequential numbers or letters assigned to the entities 1, 2, 3, … or A, B, C, … can be used to encode entities.

Significant Digit Subset Code Each digit or group of digit has its significance in this code. For example, a student's identification number is encoded as M18006, where M (first digit) stands for MCA course, 18 (second and third digits) stands for the year 2018, and the last three digits are for serial number.

Picture Coding In this coding scheme, instead of number or alphabet, an image is used to label the entities. For example, an image of star is used to indicate important entities.

Color Coding In this coding scheme, instead of number or alphabet, specific color code is used to label the entities. For example, colored dot is used to indicate vegetarian or nonvegetarian food items.

6.10.11 What Are the Objectives of Input to a System? Explain in Brief

The basic objective of input deals with the quality of the input, selection of items needed to input, and validations on them. The input mechanism must be user friendly too. The major objectives of the input are as follows:

- Correct input with proper prompted help to the users.
- Use of proper validation to avoid wrong input.

- Minimum to save time, effort, and errors; better to take ready inputs if available.
- Avoid delay.
- Collected in simple and user-friendly manner.

6.10.12 Write a Brief Note on Data Capture Guidelines

Data capture guidelines help in acquisition of required data in efficient manner. Such guidelines help in managing the data capture interfaces as well as devices, location, and mechanism to capture data. The help for data preparation, cleaning and preprocessing of data, possible validations on data, and retrieval of already existing data is also provided to the developers.

The major guidelines/considerations that may be helpful while capturing data are as follows:

- Entities to input, its availability, type, format, encoding scheme, etc. must be known prior to capturing data.
- The data can be captured at key punching at source, through online transfer, through turnaround document, through handheld terminal, etc., which may be considered here keeping a wide variety of input mechanisms in mind. That is, from which device and location input will be collected? Captured data must be clear from noise, readable, valid, and properly encoded if needed.
- How input would be given to the system: in offline or online manner? If the input is provided in offline or batch mode, is there any cleaning and preprocessing required on it?
- Is it required to codify the big and complex input in order to simplify the input procedures? If yes, what is the coding scheme?

6.10.13 Enlist Various Software Design Principles in One to Two Lines Each

Refer to Table 6.5.

6.10.14 Explain Coupling as Software Design Principle

For ease of development, control, and use, a big and complex system is divided into various modules. Coupling is defined as strength of relationship between the modules of the system. Since these modules are divided from a parent module, coupling cannot be reduced to zero. However, the degree of coupling must be low to allow the modules to be developed and to be used independently. If one module is failed, the system can still work with remaining modules with the limited functionality. To achieve this, the parameters between modules needed to be controlled, sharing of data and resources between the modules is minimized, and inter-module interactions need to be avoided.

6.10.15   What Is Cohesion? How It Can Be Increased?

Cohesion is defined as interrelationship of the instructions and structures within a module. It is a measure showing how well the module logic is built and used to serve the purpose. The elements such as instructions, data structure, and data within the modules/functions are needed to be logically related with each other at a given instance of time. The degree of cohesion must be as high as possible. See Sect. 6.8 for more details.

6.10.16   What Are the Typical Outputs of a Design Phase? Or When Design Phase of a Systems Development Is Completed, What Are the Deliverables of the Phase?

When design phase is completed, the designer is expected to produce design documents as follows:

- Structured charts.
- Data flow diagrams or UML diagrams.
- Layout charts.
- Database or file with record layouts.
- Data dictionary.
- Validation designs.
- Screen and interface design.
- Program specifications.
- List of all activities involved in the design phase.
- List of roles and responsibilities shared by personnel and development budget and plan also need to be prepared.

6.11   Objective Questions

6.11.1   System design is specifying _____ the suggested requirements can be met.

    (a)   When   (c)   What

    (b)   How   (d)   Where

6.11.2   At the beginning of the systems design, which of the following
         documents is/are available with Systems Analyst?
         (a) List of requirements   (c) List of problems
                                                 and limitations of the
                                                 current systems
         (b) Reports of feasibility tests (d) All of these
6.11.3   At the beginning of the systems design, which of the following
         documents is/are not available with Systems Analyst?
         (a) List of requirements   (c) Layout charts
         (b) Program specifications   (d) All of these
6.11.4   _____ is the element of a system that needed to be designed.
         (a) Input   (c) Interface
         (b) Output   (d) Input, output, and interface
6.11.5   Which of the following entities should be design first?
         (a) Input   (c) Output
         (b) Process   (d) Database
6.11.6   ACC_SV_2016 is the code give to a saving account of a bank
         opened in the year 2016. It is an example of _____ input
         coding scheme.
         (a) Functional coding   (c) Category coding
         (b) Significant digit   (d) None of these
              subset coding
6.11.7   Which of the following is an example of category code?
         (a) BW_TV   (c) M_Tech_2016_007
         (b) A (meant for addition)   (d) None of these
6.11.8   Which of the following is not an output device?
         (a) Pen drive   (c) Printer
         (b) Monitor   (d) None of these
6.11.9   Which of the following is not an output?
         (a) Image scanned at source   (c) Report provided
                                                 to the manager on his
                                                 monitor
         (b) Printed bill from system   (d) None of these
6.11.10 Which of the following items should not be considered as
         an input to the system?
         (a) Data that system   (c) Constant data
              can retrieve
         (b) Data that system   (d) All of these
              can calculate
6.11.11 According to the software design principles, _____
         is to be minimized.
         (a) Coupling   (c) Design effort
         (b) Cohesion   (d) All of these

6.11.12 _____ is defined as the internal strength of a module
or binding within a module of a system.
  (a) Coupling   (c) Design effort
  (b) Cohesion   (d) None of these
6.11.13 _____ is defined as strength of relationship
between the modules.
  (a) Coupling   (c) Design effort
  (b) Cohesion   (d) None of these

Answers

6.11.1	How	6.11.2	All of these
6.11.3	Program specifications	6.11.4	Input, output, and interface
6.11.5	Output	6.11.6	Significant digit subset coding
6.11.7	BW_TV	6.11.8	None of these
6.11.9	Image scanned at source	6.11.10	All of these
6.11.11	Coupling	6.11.12	Cohesion
6.11.13	Coupling		

Chapter 7
Systems Quality and Implementation Issues

Abstract The chapter discusses issues related to the systems quality and implementation as well as activities related to systems development. The chapter presents objectives for good-quality and reliable systems by giving major approaches to the systems reliability such as error avoidance, error detection and corrections, and error tolerance. The chapter also discusses possible causes of errors in the system. Various types of maintenance are also discussed in this chapter. Various methods exist to assure quality of a system, prime of which are testing, verification and validation, and certification. This chapter discusses these methods in brief. It is clear that the testing certifies the quality of a system. This chapter presents in-depth discussion on the testing techniques with various testing strategies, test data, and special systems tests. For implementation, training to the various stakeholders of the system is must. Topics such as in-house training, users training, operators training, etc. are discussed. The chapter presents a brief overview on post implementation review and methods for systems time and effort estimations. At the end of the chapter, practice questions and objective questions with answers are provided.

© Springer Nature Singapore Pte Ltd. 2017
P.S. Sajja, *Essence of Systems Analysis and Design*,
DOI 10.1007/978-981-10-5128-9_7

7.1 Introduction to Systems Quality

Providing better quality procedures has always remained a basic goal of any systems analysis and design practice. When quality of a system is thought, reliability is considered as a major quality attribute. When a system is in use, a level of reliability besides other quality attributes is expected. It is obvious that the system must not be harmful to its own users in direct or indirect way. Further, the system must give correct, required, and useful output in a predefined time period. In addition to that, output of a system must be cost-effective. The reliability directly refers to the consistent and stable output of system. It is an assurance that the system will work on demand. Reliability of a system is also expressed as Mean Time Between Failures (MTBF) or reliability coefficient. Reliability and other qualitative features of a system will be achieved through good design of the system. If basic skeleton (framework) of the system along with other components is designed properly, it results in reliable system. For example, if the manager wants the gender-wise report, design of database or file should have included the field of gender in it. Design objectives for systems reliability are enlisted in Table 7.1.

Besides the reliability, the other quality parameters such as portability, usability, user-friendliness, functionality, maintainability, and efficiency are also important. They are defined in brief as follows:

- Portability refers to an ability to adapt different infrastructure such as new machines, new platforms, and new environment from the selected one without much change.
- Usability is defined as the capability to use the output of a system for learning and problem-solving.
- User-friendliness is defined as ease of use of the system. The system developed must be easy to install, operate/navigate, and troubleshoot. The interaction

Table 7.1 Design objectives for systems reliability

Objective	Description
Correct output	The very first objective of any system toward reliability is to provide correct output
In line with users' requirements	The system must produce results which are required and demanded by users
Output in predefined time	The system must produce results in a given time. If system cannot produce results immediately, it should provide an intermediate message to users
Consistency	The system must work on demand. It should provide stable output without failure. For a situation experimented on different time, system should present same output. The systems pattern of behavior should be deviated from its standard and defined manner in similar situations over time
Safe and useful output	The system must not produce results which are harmful, costly, and impractical. Ethical, legal, and security issues must be taken care

between the system and users need not require any third-party help, at least for routine operations of the system.

- Functionality of a system is defined as an ability to perform intended functions demanded by its users.
- Maintainability of a system can be described as an ability to modify the system for corrective actions and/or future requirements.
- Efficiency of a system is the capability of a system to exhibit required performance in comparison of the resources, effort, and time utilized.

7.2 Managing Systems Reliability

To ensure a systems reliability, many approaches can be thought. One simple solution is to avoid any error in the system and develop a perfect solution. Such error avoidance is practically impossible for the big and complex real-life systems. Another approach is error detection and correction. According to the error correction and detection approach, errors of the system are identified and corrected. Obviously, earlier identification of error is always better and cheaper. While receiving the data (input), validation is also helpful while employing this approach. Another approach, called error tolerance approach, suggests to accept the errors of the system and continue with the errors after possible correction of them or omitting the errors. One can temporarily lock the modules with errors and continue with other modules of the system, if the error is not affecting the other modules of the system. For example, if the Books Issue Module in a typical library management system has a problem, a Book Return Module will always work. See Table 7.2 for the approaches to the systems reliability.

Most of the errors are resulted from the poor design. Errors at the time of programming are mainly syntactical errors, which are corrected immediately via program editors and compilers. Semantic errors in individual functions occur due to logic and poorly designed program specifications, some of which also can be corrected during unit testing. Design of system is prepared according to the requirements provided to the developers of the system. In this case, main causes of having errors in the design of the system are given below:

Table 7.2 Approaches to the systems reliability

Approach	Description
Error avoidance approach	To avoid any error in the system and develop a perfect solution, which is practically impossible for the big and complex real-life systems
Error detection and correction approach	To identify possible errors of the system and correct them; obviously, earlier is better
Error tolerance approach	To accept the errors of the system and continue with the errors after possible correction of them or omitting the errors

Table 7.3 Maintenance of a system

Maintenance	Description
Corrective maintenance	Though the system is well tested by a variety of testing techniques and special systems tests, it may cause errors and exceptions. Corrective maintenance is done to identify and solve such errors. Besides the basic error correction, the corrective maintenance also needs consideration of security aspects related to the system
Perfective maintenance	Perfective maintenance is done on a system, which is giving basic and correct result; however, it still needs an improvement. Such maintenance is needed for better interface, formatted and effective reports and other outputs from the system, reorganization and fine-tuning of results by the system, and making the system more responsive. This type of maintenance is generally done immediately after performing corrective maintenance
Adaptive maintenance	Adaptive maintenance is a kind of systems maintenance, where systems procedures and software are changed to accommodate new requirements, changed platform, new infrastructure, and changed working environment. Generally such maintenance is required at the time of systems upgrade or hardware infrastructure improvement. This type of maintenance will come after long-time use of a system

- *Not obtaining the right requirements from users*: It may be possible that the users are not aware of the system's working. The system may be really innovative in nature, or users are not willing to provide requirements because of the lack of knowledge or have developed fear/bias against the system such as losing the job. It may be possible that the proper target users might not have been identified by Systems Analyst. Generally users are not proactive in nature; hence, they may not come up themselves with right requirements.
- *Not getting the requirements in the right manner*: The requirements provided by the users may not be understood properly. There may be many reasons for that. First of all, users do not know how to represent the requirements in proper form/ words. Further, the Systems Analyst may not have the domain knowledge and particularly domain taxonomy and jargons. Because of these reasons, the interpretation of the requirements provided by users may be totally different when the requirements reach to the Systems Analyst's desk.
- *Not translating the requirements in clear and understandable manner*: It is Systems Analyst's duty to encourage users to suggest requirements for the system. Further, understanding the requirements is also one of the responsibilities of the Systems Analyst. If the Systems Analyst has understood the requirements properly, he would pass them to the module leaders, programmers, and testers. Rightly conveying the requirements to the developers (such as programmers and testers) leads to the required development of the system. That is, the users will get the required systems, if their requirements are properly communicated and understood at every level, by the Analysts, by the programmers, and by the testers.

7.3 Systems Maintainability

Previous section has discussed the causes of the errors; many of them are due to poor design of the system. If the systems design is proper, quality of the system will be of acceptable level. Further, the resulting system is easy to use and maintain. Otherwise the system will immediately need maintenance. Table 7.3 enlists three major types of maintenance of a system.

7.4 Systems/Software Quality Assurance

The software along with its necessary documentation must be of some acceptable level of quality. The quality of software and its related documentation must be up to the mark and should meet necessary standards. The quality of the system/software is assured by verifying the quality parameters such as correctness, reliability, maintainability, completeness, etc. Various activities such as testing, validation and verification, and certification help in verifying the level of quality of the given system. This section briefly describes these concepts. Also see Table 7.4 which enlists the quality assurance techniques in brief.

Testing Testing of a system is a very important activity among various activities related to the systems development. Testing is critical to certify the quality of a system. It is a kind of assurance given to the system. Testing of a system is costly and effort taking but guarantees a level of quality for the system. It is better to test system as early as possible, even if the system is not fully developed. See Sect. 7.5 for the detailed discussion on testing techniques, strategies, and preparation of testing data.

Table 7.4 Quality assurance techniques

Quality assurance technique	Description
Testing	Different components of design and code of the system should be tested in various ways. Unit testing, systems testing, and special systems tests should be performed on the system
Validation and verification (V&V)	Verification is the process of finding errors in a simulated environment, generally by the internal users, whereas the validation checks for errors in live or external environment. Further, validation also validates the data if errors are found
Certification	Standards defined by organizations at national and international levels (or custom defined by the organization itself) are applied on system to ensure quality of system. An organization (where system is being developed or used) may appoint its own team of specialists to test and certify quality of the system

Validation and Verification Verification is the process of finding errors. Validation also checks for errors, but here the environment of execution of the system is live. Further, validation also corrects (validates) the data if errors are found. Verification of system is done within a simulated environment and generally to its internal or limited users. Hence, it is also known as alpha testing by some users. On the other hand, beta testing puts system in front of external users, generally for live test. Validation can be a little long process as it involves a big and live audience for testing of the system. As a result of validation, there may be correction in software, and new patchwork for the system may be developed to recover the bugs or errors found.

Certification Some organizations at national and international levels have defined acceptable standards of quality of a system. To ensure quality of system, help of some standards can be taken. If system satisfies the requirement of well-defined standards, quality of the system is ensured. If the system is really novel and matching quality standards are not available, in that case, the organization may propose a suitable set of standards. The organization (where system is being developed or used) may appoint a team of specialists to test and certify quality of the system.

7.5 Testing

As discussed in the previous section, testing is an important activity to ensure quality of a system. Not only code but all the deliverables and outputs at different phases of systems analysis and design are required to be tested. The following lists show possible items to test:

- Testing can start very early with the cross verification of requirements listed in requirements specification provided by users and Systems Analysts.
- Once design of the system is prepared, the design also should be cross verified with the available set of requirements. It is also needed to be checked that design is feasible to develop further or not. The design diagrams and specifications are also needed to be checked.
- Code developed from the program specification is also needed to be checked thoroughly by considering all possible cases with variety of sample test cases. Generally code for a module is tested separately, and later it is integrated with the other modules to form a big system. On a full-fledged system, further testing is also done. Testing a code for module is known as *unit testing*, and testing the full system (or bigger component) is known as an *integrated testing* or *systems testing*. Unit testing can be performed in top-down as well as bottom-up ways. In bottom-up way, testing is started with the smallest (lowest-level) module and progressing toward the upper level using drivers. In case of top-down approach, it begins with the highest (upper)-level module and proceeds toward lower-level modules using temporary results or stubs. Testing experts also use the words glass box testing and black box testing. Here black box testing refers to the testing technique of software without the knowledge of source code within the mod-

Table 7.5 Special systems tests

Special systems tests	Description
Peak load test	Tests whether system can take load of the maximum volume of activities without error and meets the expectation
Transaction performance test	The transactions of the system must be performed efficiently, especially considering the time and cost
Storage test	Tests the capacity of the system to store information related to users and transactions
Recovery and backup tests	Tests the chances of recovery in case of the accidental loss of data or failure of system. It also verifies about the backup of the data as well as software
Procedure tests	Tests whether the main line business functions are carried out properly by the system or not. It also checks the run time procedures, error-handling procedures, and other control procedures
Human factor test	Tests the usability and friendliness of the system and verifies if users of the system are comfortable with the system or not

ule. On the contrary, glass box testing refers to the testing strategy with complete knowledge of code and structure within the module. The glass box testing is also known as "clear box" or "open box" testing. The black box testing can be applied at many levels of the system, viz., unit level, module level, and systems level.

- *Regressive testing* can also be done on the system to verify that the old software/ procedures of the system still run with new changes in the system.
- The system must be tested against its maximum capacity in terms of data handling, users, and performance of transactions. *Special systems tests* such as range and limit test on a field, peak load testing, storage testing, performance time testing, recover and backup testing, and procedure testing can be designed to test the system thoroughly. Table 7.5 discusses such special systems tests in brief.

Test Data To test the system, data are needed. One way to get the data is to take it from live environment. This approach of getting data for testing is called *live test data*. Live environment is a very good source of the typical and routine data. However, it is risky to put the system into live environment before complete testing. Another alternative is to use the dummy data created by experts of the field. If designed properly, dummy data of wide variety from different aspects of the system can test the system thoroughly. Such *artificial test data* encompasses all possible combinations of values for testing purpose. Further, it eliminates the need of putting the system in a live environment before testing. This is the reason why most of the time, Systems Analysts or dedicated testers of the system prefer the artificial test data. Third alternative is to use the readymade and *reusable library* or *standard set of data*. It can be organization-wide test library prepared by the organization itself with the help of team of experts. Such library is reusable and common for many systems. Many organizations have created such test libraries and made them available at common public place such as Web platform. Such commonly available test libraries are generic in nature and can be used for many systems. Publicly available large data set for testing should be machine readable or uses a universal format such as comma-separated values, Extensible Markup Language (XML), and Attribute-Relation File Format (ARFF).

7.6 Systems Implementation Issues

Once working of the system is tested properly, the implementation procedure begins. Before implementation of the system, training to the vendors, users, and systems operators is provided. The training schedules, trainers, and sample data with necessary tools and support structure are planned and prepared, and training is derived. After training, the old system is converted into a new system. Working of the new system is measured through post implementation review. The post implementation review highlights the need of maintenance and leads us toward the next cycle of analysis and design of the same system. The training, conversion, and post implementation review topics are discussed in this section.

7.6.1 Training

Operation of a system needs an orientation about how to use the system. The system may be highly user friendly and operationally feasible, even though many users face a starting trouble. Training removes this hurdle and encourages users to use the system in proper manner. For example, though many people drive car, they might not know about the standard way to start a car or change a gear as well as how to use seat belt! Many people would realize it later that if the seat belt of a front seat of a car is not fasten properly, the airbags won't come out in an emergency. At least a word is needed to make them aware about the systematic use of the resources in order to get maximum benefit from the system.

Training of the system can be given in different ways to different users. There are hands-on end users or *systems operators*, to whom training should be given about how the basic and routine operations of the system are carried out. Data entry, installation of new tool or machine, to run or to stop procedures, and other operations are generally involved in systems operators training. Also, such users must be made aware of exceptional situations, so that they can handle systems operations in efficient way. Systems operators are responsible for managing access rights to the various types of users and must be trained for handling and creating new groups of users. Further, the systems operators are responsible for creating instruction manuals for common users to help them in routine operations.

In case of common users training, they are made aware of routine operations of the system only. Use of tools, calling typical procedures, creating reports from transactions, and proper initiation and shutdown of the systems training will be given to the common users.

7.6.2   Training Methods

Training requires the developed system, equipment, and data along with a willing audience to be trained. Many times the systems setup and the procedures are common in nature and require generic infrastructural facilities. In that case, many users and systems operators are called at one common place, and training should be given. The person involved in the development or setup (vendor or Systems Analysts) of the system often becomes the trainer. That is why the preferable location for such training is location of vendors or developers. Alternatively, it can be a common location where trainee as well a trainer can approach easily. This is known as vendor site training. Such training is provided as part of purchase or development of the system; hence, it is called *vendor and in-service training.*

Location, where the system is going to be implemented, plays an important role also. If the system is infrastructure specific (i.e., the system uses application-specific infrastructure), it will become necessary to provide training on the site where system would be implemented. Here training should be much customized according to the infrastructure and requirements of the users. This is known as *in-house training.* Training regarding tailor made system and infrastructure will be provided here.

7.6.3   Conversion

At this stage, system is ready, and users are also trained and ready to use the new system. This is the high time to make effective use of the system. This is the time to shift to the new system. If there is any old system running, it can be continued, and in parallel, new system is used. This gives us double surety and minimum risk from failure of the new system but wastes time and effort in managing two systems in parallel. This approach is known as *parallel approach.*

One bold step can be directly switching over to the new system and stop working with the old system. This is risky, as the new system may fail. But, if successful, immediate benefits of new technology and better procedures can be ensured. This approach is suitable if the new system is well tested and reliable. This is known as *direct cutover.*

It is also possible to implement a working version (prototype) of system into part of an organization, and feedback is invited. Based on the feedback, the system is improved, and in other parts of the organization, the system will be implemented. This is a kind of live test of a system within an organization; however, other sections of the organizations may feel that the system is still incomplete. This approach is known as *pilot approach.*

One more alternative to implement system is to consider a perfectly developed part of system and implement it across the whole organization. This saves resources and offers incremental implementation of the system. However, it disappoints users due to time taking and long phase-in time. This approach is known as *phase-in* approach.

Before actual systems conversion, careful and detailed planning is needed to first choose the appropriate method for conversion and later the activities during the conversion process. The very first activity in conversion planning is to determine person/team responsible for the conversion activities. Such conversion team with *conversion manager*, as the head of the team, controls and monitors the conversion processes. Typical activities in the conversion planning are to take care about the systems procedures/working systems model, documentation and manuals, tools needed for implementation, data preparation for actual demonstration, and site preparation.

7.6.4   Post Implementation Review

To know about the systems performance after its implementation, post implementation review is carried out. All fact-finding methods such as questionnaire, interview, record review, and observation techniques are useful here. Besides these techniques, opinion/sentiment analysis, attitude survey, and walk-through on systems documents and deliverables can also be considered for post implementation review. The Systems Analyst along with his committee may prepare some review questions about the various aspects of the systems performance. Some aspects to prepare such review questions are given below:

- Major functions of system are performing well and according to expectations.
- Systems output quality is up to the predetermined standard and acceptable.
- Friendly and easy use of system.
- Benefits of the system toward users and organization; cost, effort, profit, productivity, brand image of the organization, overall impact of the system, etc. can be considered here.
- Requirement of maintenance, if any with justification.

7.7   Methods for Systems Development Time Estimation

Successful management of systems development activities and resulting system can be done via monitoring and controlling resources, time, tasks, and requirements of the users. It is observed that time requirement for carrying out analysis, design, and testing (each) is generally between 20 and 35% of the total systems development time. Ideally 30–40% of the total development time should be given to the testing; however, it may not be possible always. The following are the common time estimation methods:

- *Historical Method for Time Estimation*: Based on the history records and documents available in the organization, time and effort can be estimated, according to which systems development activities can be planned.

- *Intuitive Method for Time Estimation*: An expert of systems development activities may determine the suitable time and effort requirements for the systems development activities based on his insight and experience. This is the most common method for time estimation.
- *Standard Arithmetic Formula Method for Time Estimation*: This approach has strong base of logic. Parameters that affect the systems development process such as nature of the system, complexity of the system, size of the system, resources available, etc. are identified, and based on these parameters, a weighted formula may be prepared. This formula is then used to estimate project time, effort, and cost.

Along with the suitable time management method mentioned above, various tools for time management such as function point analysis, calendar time requirements, bar charts, PERT/CPM, milestone chart, etc. are helpful.

7.8 Practice Questions

7.8.1 List Down the Parameters Used to Evaluate Quality of a System. Explain Each in Brief

The very first thing about the systems quality is expectation of correct answers in the given time. After that, parameters like reliability and efficiency come as major quality factors. Reliability, efficiency, and other quality parameters are described in Sect. 7.1 of this chapter. Brief summary is given in a tabular form as follows (Table 7.6).

Table 7.6 Parameters of systems quality

Reliability	Assurance that the system is not harmful to its users and provides necessary solutions in a given time as per the expectations
Efficiency	Capability of a system to exhibit required performance in comparison of the resources, effort, and time utilized
Portability	An ability to adapt different infrastructures such as new machines, new platforms, and new environment
Usability	Capability to use the output of a system for learning and problem-solving
User-friendliness	Ease of use, ease of installing and troubleshooting the system, particularly for typical routine operations
Functionality	Ability of the system to perform intended functions demanded and meet the requirements
Maintainability	Ability to modify the system for corrective actions and adaption of future requirements/platform/infrastructure

7.8.2   Define Reliability of a System. How a Degree of Reliability Is Measured for an Information System?

Reliability refers to the quality of a system, which ensures that the system is not harmful to its users. It also ensures the required output to its users in a given time and specified environment. By this way, assurance of consistent and stable output of system to its user is provided. Reliability is a factor that specifies a level of guarantee to its users about the systems satisfactory operations along with its total infrastructure (including hardware and software). Reliability of a system is also expressed as Mean Time Between Failures (MTBF) or reliability coefficient. Refer to Table 7.1 for detail.

7.8.3   Discuss the Design Objectives for Systems Reliability

The design objectives for systems reliability are enlisted below.

Correct Output The system must provide correct output to its users.

In Line with Users' Requirements The system must produce outputs which are demanded by users and are in line with the basic objective of the system.

Output in Predefined Time The system must produce results in an expected time. For example, a photocopier machine should give you copy of a text page within a few seconds; if not, it should provide some error message or signal (red light).

Consistency The system must provide stable output every time. In similar situations experienced at different time, the output must be similar.

Safe and Useful Output The system should produce correct, acceptable (technically, operationally, legally, and ethically) decisions/outputs.

7.8.4   What Are the Approaches of Systems Reliability? Explain in Brief

The broad approaches of systems reliability are as follows:

1. Avoid errors in system and try to build ideal and complete system, which is not practically possible.
2. Identify all possible errors within the system, as early as possible, and correct.
3. Accept the errors of the system, if possible validate them, and continue working with systems.

7.8.5 Explain Various Causes of the Errors in the Design of a System

The following are the main causes of having errors in the design of the system:

1. Not obtaining the right requirements from users
2. Not getting the requirements in the right manner
3. Not translating the requirements in clear and understandable manners

For discussion refer to Sect. 7.2.

7.8.6 Define the Following Terms: (1) Corrective Maintenance, (2) Perfective Maintenance, and (3) Adaptive Maintenance

Corrective Maintenance Corrective maintenance is done to identify and solve any errors from the output of the system. Besides the error correction, improvement in security aspects of the system may also be considered here.

Perfective Maintenance The systems output may be correct, but may not be presentable or in desired format. Efforts are needed to improve the presentation, interface, and effectiveness of the output provided by the system. It is a kind of fine-tuning of results by the system. Perfective maintenance is generally done immediately after the corrective maintenance.

Adaptive Maintenance Such maintenance is done to adopt new requirements or platform/infrastructure. Generally, after successful delivery and utilization of the system, such maintenance is needed to keep the system up to date.

7.8.7 How the Necessary Quality Level of a System Is Assured? Explain in Detail

Quality can be result of good analysis and design process; however, it only certified by testing. As said anonymously, testing is one of the major quality controls. The process of *testing* may take some time, cost, and effort; however, it ensures users for systems operations. Testing may start in parallel with coding; immediately after developing a small function/utility, it should be tested. Besides live data, test case libraries, standard generic data sets, and customized data sets are used to test the system. See Sect. 7.5 for detailed discussion on testing techniques, strategies, and preparation of testing data.

While encoding the system, *validation and verification* can also be carried out to ensure reliability of the system. Generally, verification is the process of finding errors. Validation too checks for errors, however, in live environment and validates the data if errors are found. For this, a simulated environment is generated if application is not ready completely. As verification first given to its internal users or limited users, it is sometimes known as alpha testing. As stated in the Sect. 7.5, beta testing puts system in front of external users, generally for live testing. Validation may take little longer time. To recover the bugs or errors found during validation process, the software may undergo some changes.

Besides the abovementioned factors (testing, verification and validations), certification is another attribute that provides a kind of assurance about systems operations to its users. There are many standards provided by national and international organizations related to software development. The system may use customized standards defined by the organization itself, particularly for novel type of systems.

7.8.8   Discuss Various Testing Practices and Items to Be Tested While Developing an Information System

The following are the major considerations while performing testing:

- Testing ideally should start very early, by verifying the requirements and feasibility reports on the requirements listed.
- Similarly the design documents are also tested against the valid requirements enlisted.
- As soon as a utility/code is developed, it has to be tested. Code developed from the program specification is also needed to be checked thoroughly by considering all possible cases with variety of sample test cases.
- Generally code for a module is tested separately (unit testing), and later it is integrated with the other modules to form a big system, which is called integrated testing.
- Testing can be performed in top-down as well as bottom-up ways. In bottom-up way, testing is started with the smallest (lowest-level) module and progressing toward the upper level using drivers. In case of top-down approach, it begins with the highest (upper)-level module and proceeds toward lower-level modules using temporary results or stubs. These strategies are also known as glass box testing and black box testing. In black box testing, the module is tested without the knowledge of source code within the module. On the contrary, glass box testing tests the module with complete knowledge of code and structure within it. The glass box testing is also known as "clear box" or "open box" testing. The black box testing can be applied at many levels of the system, viz., unit level, module level, and systems level.
- Regressive testing can also be done on the system to verify that the system still run with new changes in the system.

The system must be tested against its maximum capacity in terms of data handling, users, and performance of transactions. Special systems tests such as range and limit test on a field, peak load testing, storage testing, performance time testing, recover and backup testing, and procedure testing can be designed to test the system thoroughly.

The items to be tested are requirements and other outputs from analysis phase, design documents such as diagrams and specifications, code of modules of the system, and test data themselves. Even after successful implementation and use of the system, post implementation testing and review can be done.

7.8.9 Discuss Special Systems Tests

Besides typical unit testing and integrated testing, following special systems test may be carried out on the system:

Peak Load Test To test that the system can take load of the maximum volume of activities and performs well.

Transaction Performance Test To test how the systems operations/transactions are carried out in expected time and quality.

Storage Test To test storage capacity of the system for transactions and user-/product-/service-related information.

Recovery and Backup Tests To test how well the recovery of data is handled and periodical backup is ensured by the system or not.

Procedure Tests To test whether the core operations of the business are supported by the system or not. As stated in the chapter, it also checks the run time procedures, error-handling procedures, and other control procedures.

Human Factor Test To test the usability and friendliness of the system.
    Refer to Table 7.5.

7.8.10 Describe (1) Unit Testing and (2) Systems Testing

System is divided into module for ease of development and use. Each module of the system is developed and tested individually. Testing can be performed in top-down as well as bottom-up ways. Testing a code for module/unit is called unit testing. In bottom-up way, testing is started with the smallest (lowest-level) module and progressing toward the upper level using drivers. In case of top-down approach, it begins with the highest (upper)-level module and proceeds toward lower-level modules using temporary/hypothetical results.

Once all the units are tested properly, they are integrated to build a complete system. Testing the resulting integrated system is known as an integrated testing or systems testing for its intended goal and objectives.

Refer to Sect. 7.5.

7.8.11   How Test Data Can Be Arranged to Test a System? Discuss in Detail

Test data for the system can be managed in three major ways as follows:

1. *Live test data*: System is set in live environment to perform operations for real business. Live and actual data are fed to the system. This type of testing is risky, as the errors during systems operations may result in creating false brand image of the system.
2. *Dummy data*: Dummy data are laboratory-generated data by considering all major aspects of the business. If created well, it checks majority of situations that may happen while using the systems. In reality only a typical (popular) situation occurs frequently, which may not incorporate exceptional data. On other hand, laboratory data may have included exceptional cases also.
3. *Test libraries*: There are readymade, reusable generic libraries or standard sets of data available in common acceptable format. Publicly available such large data set for testing should be machine readable or documented in a universal format such as comma-separated values, Extensible Markup Language (XML), and Attribute-Relation File Format (ARFF). These data sets might have undergone various checking and revisions to ensure proper testing of system.

7.8.12   Define Users Training and Systems Operators Training. Also State the Difference Between These Two

Systems Operators Training   Such training is given to the systems operators about the basic and routine operations of the system. Operations such as data entry, installation of new tool or machine, to run or to stop procedures, handling exceptional situations, etc. are generally involved.

Common Users Training   Common users are given training about routine operations of the system generally. Use of tools, calling typical procedures, creating reports from transactions, and proper initiation and shutdown of the systems training will be given to the common users.

The main differences between both the methods are given in Table 7.7.

Table 7.7 Systems operators training and users training

Systems operators training	Users training
Besides common and routine operations, the systems operators are given training for installing, troubleshooting, and removing (de-installation) of the system	Users are made aware of common and routine operations training
Detailed knowledge of exceptional situations and troubleshooting training is given	Overview of exceptional situations is given to common users
Information about the access rights to the various types of users is provided with training for handling and creating new groups of users	No such information is given except password creating and strength about password hints
Systems operators are responsible for creating instructional manuals for common users to help them in routine operations	No such responsibility is given to common users. However, they are responsible for valid use of the systems procedures and infrastructure

7.8.13 In Which Situation In-House Training Is Useful?

If the system is infrastructure specific (i.e., the system uses application-specific or customized infrastructure), it will become necessary to provide training on the site where system would be implemented. Here training should be customized according to the infrastructure and requirements of the users.

7.8.14 Explain in Detail the Four Approaches of Conversion? Can We Mix Any of These Approaches? Explain with an Example

The four approaches of converting an old system into the new system and making the new system in use are listed below:

- Parallel approach
- Direct cutover approach
- Pilot approach
- Phase in

We can hybridize these approaches on need, for example, a phase of a system can be experimented in parallel with the existing system.

The approaches are discussed in Sect. 7.6.

7.8.15   Define Role and Responsibilities of Conversion Manager

The very first activity in conversion planning is to determine person/team responsible for the conversion activities. Such conversion team with *conversion manager*, as the head of the team, controls and monitors the conversion processes. The typical activities in the conversion planning are as follows:

- To make team members aware about their roles and responsibilities
- To take care about the systems procedures/working systems model, documentation and manuals, and tools needed for implementation
- To prepare venue and data for actual demonstration
- To handle and deliver the software, hardware, documentation, and related assistance during implementation as well as training

The conversion manager is responsible in making plan for conversion, taking care of the problem that arises during the conversion of system, and assigning and administrating the responsibilities and roles to the subordinates during the conversion process.

7.8.16   What Are the Typical Problems That May Arise While Converting an Old System into New System? How Can They Be Handled?

During conversion of an old system into the new system, the following possible problems may occur:

- Missing procedural documents, manuals, or corrupted software/hardware (CDs or pen drive may not work).
- Operating platform, software versions, and hardware may not match.
- Mismatched data formats between current and new files.
- Errors in data translation.
- Missing data or lost files.
- Situations that were overlooked during systems development (e.g., data are missing, not in required format, or need to be cleared or preprocessed).
- Permission and access rights for accessing venue and infrastructure use may not be taken.

Such problems may be handled by careful planning and managing the activities related to the conversion process. One can do the following:

- Prepare list of roles and responsibilities, and assign responsibility for each activity.
- Prepare a detailed plan regarding the conversion activities.

- Prepare a list of files, necessary infrastructure, and data required with necessary encoding, validation, and preprocessing.
- Collect all documents and procedures.
- Prepare a checklist of all controls/operations to be used.
- Ensure procedures for cross-checking and comparing the old and new systems.
- Verify conversion schedules and conversion site along with any permission needed such as gate pass.

7.8.17 Explain Methods and Tools Useful in Post Implementation Reviews

Post implementation review is carried out to know about the new systems performance. For this, standard fact-finding methods such as interviews, questionnaire, interview, record review, and observation are used. One may go for opinion/sentiment analysis, attitude survey, and walk-through on systems documents and deliverables. Systems Analyst along with his committee may prepare some review questions about the various aspects of the systems performance.

7.8.18 What Is the Importance of Time Estimation of a System? What Benefits Does It Offer?

Proper estimations of the systems facilitate a sound plan to carry out for systems development activities. Resources, time, tasks, and requirements of the users are well managed through proper plan of the development. Further, it also ensures that no important activities will be missed or overlooked. Time and effort estimation for various phases of systems development helps in monitoring and controlling the systems development activities.

7.8.19 Explain Methods of Time and Effort Estimation for Developing an Information Systems Project

The following are the common time and effort estimation methods:

- *Historical Method for Time Estimation*: Based on the history records and documents.
- *Intuitive Method for Time Estimation*: Based on the developers' insight and experience.

- *Standard Arithmetic Formula Method for Time Estimation*: Based on an arithmetic formula incorporating the critical parameters that affect the systems development process (nature of the system, complexity of the system, size of the system, etc.).
- *With Standard General Tools*: Tools such as function point analysis, calendar time requirements, bar charts, PERT/CPM, milestone chart, etc. can be used for time and effort estimation.

7.9 Objective Questions

7.9.1 Reliability of a system is often expressed as _____.
   - (a) Mean Time Between Failures (MTBF)
   - (c) Both Mean Time Between Failures (MTBF) and reliability coefficient
   - (b) Reliability coefficient
   - (d) None of these

7.9.2 Which of the following is not a quality-related attribute for systems development?
   - (a) Reliability
   - (c) User-friendliness
   - (b) Portability
   - (d) None of these

7.9.3 _____ of a system can be described as an ability to modify the system for corrective actions and/or future requirements.
   - (a) Maintainability
   - (c) Portability
   - (b) Interoperability
   - (d) Reliability

7.9.4 Which of the following are approaches toward systems reliability?
   - (a) Error avoidance
   - (c) Error tolerance
   - (b) Error detection and correction
   - (d) All of these

7.9.5 During _____ maintenance, systems procedures and software are changed to accommodate new requirements, changed platform, infrastructure, and working environment.
   - (a) Corrective
   - (c) Perfective
   - (b) Adaptive
   - (d) All of these

7.9.6 For better interface, formatted and effective reports and other outputs from the system, etc., _____ type of maintenance is required.
   - (a) Corrective
   - (c) Perfective
   - (b) Adaptive
   - (d) Any of these

7.9.7 Which of the following is not a quality assurance technique?
   - (a) Certification
   - (c) Testing
   - (b) Validations and verification
   - (d) Designing

7.9.8 _____ type of testing is done on each module.
   (a) Unit   (c) Integrated
   (b) Alpha   (d) Beta

7.9.9 _____ testing can also be done on the system to verify that
the old software/procedures of the system still run with new changes
in the system.
   (a) Unit   (c) Regressive
   (b) Alpha   (d) Any of these

7.9.10 _____ is an example of a special systems test.
   (a) Unit test   (c) Peak load test
   (b) Module test   (d) Integrated test

7.9.11 Acceptability of a system is mainly dependent on _____.
   (a) Programmers' effort   (c) User interface
   (b) Users' requirements   (d) Cohesion of modules

7.9.12 The testing of software module, without the knowledge of source code
within it, is called _____.
   (a) Glass box testing   (c) Black box testing
   (b) Special systems test   (d) Peak load testing

7.9.13 The testing technique that requires devising test cases to exercise
the internal logic of a software module is called _____.
   (a) Black box testing   (c) Glass box testing
   (b) Special systems testing   (d) Blind testing

7.9.14 _____ is the special systems test that determines the time
duration to process transaction data.
   (a) Peak load testing   (c) Unit testing
   (b) Performance   (d) Recovery testing
       time testing

7.9.15 Systems efficiency is defined as _____.
   (a) Doing the thing   (c) Doing right thing
       in right way   in right way
   (b) Doing right thing   (d) Any of these

7.9.16 Systems effectiveness is defined as _____.
   (a) Doing the right thing   (c) Doing thing in right way
       in right way
   (b) Doing right thing   (d) Any of these

7.9.17 From where test data (to test the system) are made available?
   (a) Live environment   (c) Dummy data
   (b) Test libraries   (d) All of these

7.9.18 _____ requires training of the new system developed.
   (a) Users   (c) Vendors
   (b) Systems operators   (d) All of these

7.9.19 _____ approach of systems conversion gives double security
with minimum amount of risk but causes high effort and time.
   (a) Direct   (c) Prototype
   (b) Parallel   (d) None of these

7.9.20 _____ is responsible to plan and manage the conversion
       (converting old system into new system) activities.
       (a) Module leader   (c) Conversion manager
       (b) Tester   (d) User manager
7.9.21 To conduct post implementation review, _____
       methods are used.
       (a) Interview   (c) Questionnaire
       (b) Observation   (d) All of these
7.9.22 Ideally the _____ phase of the systems development from
       the phases given below requires maximum efforts.
       (a) Testing   (c) Feasibility checking
       (b) Documentation   (d) All of these

Answers

7.9.1	Both Mean Time Between Failures (MTBF) and reliability coefficient	7.9.2	None of these
7.9.3	Maintainability	7.9.4	All of these
7.9.5	Adaptive	7.9.6	Perfective
7.9.7	Designing	7.9.8	Unit
7.9.9	Regressive	7.9.10	Peak load test
7.9.11	User interface	7.9.12	Black box testing
7.9.13	Glass box testing	7.9.14	Performance time testing
7.9.15	Doing the thing in right way	7.9.16	Doing right thing
7.9.17	All of these	7.9.18	All of these
7.9.19	Parallel	7.9.20	Conversion manager
7.9.21	All of these	7.9.22	Testing

Printed in the United States
By Bookmasters